IT HAPPENED IN
SOUTHERN
CALIFORNIA

IT HAPPENED IN

SOUTHERN CALIFORNIA

Stories of Events and People That
SHAPED GOLDEN STATE HISTORY

Third Edition

NOELLE SULLIVAN

Globe
Pequot   GUILFORD, CONNECTICUT

Globe Pequot

An imprint of Globe Pequot, the trade division of
The Rowman & Littlefield Publishing Group, Inc.
4501 Forbes Blvd., Ste. 200
Lanham, MD 20706
www.rowman.com

Distributed by NATIONAL BOOK NETWORK

British Library Cataloguing in Publication Information available

Library of Congress Cataloging-in-Publication Data available

ISBN 978-1-4930-6026-9 (paper)
ISBN 978-1-4930-6027-6 (electronic)

♾™ The paper used in this publication meets the minimum requirements of
American National Standard for Information Sciences—Permanence of Paper
for Printed Library Materials, ANSI/NISO Z39.48-1992

CONTENTS

CONTENTS

CONTENTS

ACKNOWLEDGMENTS

My thanks go to anyone who reads this book, curious to learn more about California; to my husband, Tim Daley, and our lovely daughters; to my friends Lee, Larkin, Lila, Greg, Mike, Liz, Pableaux, Kate, Julie, and Jen; my mother Patricia Sullivan; editor Allen Jones; and to the many people behind the scenes who helped make this little book more than a collection of notes.

INTRODUCTION

Southern California is too complex a place to be defined solely by its geography. In his landmark book *Southern California Country* (1946), Carey McWilliams wrote that the Southland begins on the sunny side of the transverse Tehachapi Range that keeps the cold from Santa Barbara. "The air is softer, the ocean is bluer, and the skies have a lazy and radiant warmth," he said of a land that still boasts of those things. Southern California is also a changed place from when he knew it, its scrubland now burdened with cars and tract homes.

It is still an environment of glamour, both natural and human-made. There is more variety in Southern California than in regions twice its size. It has beaches and ski hills, cities and wilderness. People drive at manic speeds, and relax as no one else can. The landscape is variegated as are the populations. If you do not like what you've found here, drive a few miles in either direction.

In this book of capsule histories, I've included stories from south of the Tehachapi line. I've also added tales from the state's eastern half—the Imperial Valley, Owens Valley,

Death Valley—which isn't typically considered part of the region. These areas share the same dry climate, though, and relate to the coastal metro basin. The vignettes included here are by no means the only or even the best tales the Southland has to tell. They merely hint at California's rich past and point to its varied peoples.

Telling the past is risky business in Southern California, the land of constant reinvention. Yet, as the saying goes, "Those who do not remember history are doomed to repeat it." It benefits us all to learn the best tales the Inland Empire has to offer, to learn the songs of the Southland, and to send our own music back out over the waves.

1600s

Big Bears and Basketmakers

As the Cahuilla Indian women worked in the clearing below, the boy pushed through oak and mountain cherry brush toward the ridge. He had helped his mother and her sisters gather the acorns that they now shelled and pounded into small pieces, beginning the process that would make the brown-capped nuts into something good to eat. After a few days of grinding the nuts, the women of the Wildcat clan would leach the bitter acorn flour through willow filters until it became a flavorful paste. This was the boy's favorite food, and with other seeds, dried berries, and fresh game it would feed his family's band through much of the winter.

Early in the day, the women of the mountain Cahuilla had brought out their wide, finely woven baskets and filled them with acorns, leaving the boy to explore nearby ravines. Too large to be carried in a cradleboard and too small to travel with the men, he was free to wander. He held his small bow ready as he made a winding path along the ridge, hunting rabbits. In the shade of a tall pine, the boy saw something much larger: a great brown grizzly bear.

Bears were not for hunting—they were the Cahuilla's relatives, as anyone could tell by their humanlike movements. A startled bear would stand up and gesture with its arms just like a man; mother bears showed ferocity in protecting their children, as Cahuilla women did. Since the time long ago when the world was chaos, bears and basketmakers had lived together in these mountains. Although the bears had a spirit-soul and could understand language—the boy knew this from his elders—this did not make them less dangerous. An angry bear was worse than an angry grandfather, since a bear's long curved claws and powerful muscles could kill in one paw swipe.

The big bear had been digging for ants at the base of the ponderosa pine, and the boy could see a raised hump between its shoulders. The bear had seen him first, though. Now it reared up on both hind feet and shook its massive head from side to side. The boy froze in fear, but did as he had been taught. "Piwil, Great-Grandfather," he said in a soft, diplomatic tone. "I am only looking for my food. Since you are human and understand me, take my word and go away."

The bear tried to say something back, opening its snout and chuffing at the person who had so rudely interrupted its foraging.

"Please, my relative. I mean you no harm," the boy added. It took all his energy to stand still, to keep from darting through the brush.

At last, the bear shook its head and dropped to the ground. Then, to the boy's great relief, it ambled away.

We have no written records of those days, so we cannot prove that this story is true. We can only imagine that the boy's mother was proud of his prudent action, and that she used dyed grasses to weave parts of the story—oak leaves, rabbits, winding trails—into her next basket. Similarly ornamented and tightly coiled baskets, often with an amazing 133 stitches per inch, are among the best legacies we have of the Cahuilla people who lived in Southern California long before later settlers did. Fewer than a thousand Cahuilla descendants live in the Southland today. They have preserved their ancestors' beautiful baskets and other pieces of the historic Cahuilla culture at the Malki Museum of the Morongo Reservation.

California grizzlies, now extinct, have left no records. But their former presence here lives on in Cahuilla stories and in the name of Big Bear Lake, which rests high in the San Bernardino Mountains.

1769

Scurvy's Harbor

The cry went up at sunset—white sails on the horizon! The *San Carlos* had arrived at last. Captain Juan Pérez and his crew aboard the *San Antonio* had been waiting at the rendezvous point in San Diego Bay for weeks, fearing their partners had been lost at sea. Now the missing ship sailed into the fishhook-shaped harbor just as the sun dropped below the waterline. It was too dark to board the *San Carlos* that night, but all aboard the *San Antonio* celebrated the happy reunion.

Their glad yells faded the next morning when they saw no signs of activity aboard the *San Carlos* in the bay. The ship had dropped no shore boat from its hull, and its sails were still unfurled for travel. Pérez used his looking glass but could see no one on board. Something clearly was wrong.

Pérez's men rowed over and found a ship of the dead and the living dead.

The *San Carlos* was loaded with supplies for founding a new Catholic mission. It also carried the sailor's worst enemy—scurvy. The crew of the *San Antonio* boarded the ship and were horrified by what they found. All aboard the San Carlos were in awful condition, and twenty-four had died in the last week. Those who were still alive could barely move. The mysterious illness seemed to be a kind of decay in the veins. It broke out as sores on the men's flesh, swelling their gums and soft tissues to the bleeding point. It weakened them and depressed their spirits. Every touch was painful. Some sailors were so affected they could not move or eat the beef jerky and hardtack that was their fare.

The twenty-eight sailors from the *San Antonio* had also had early signs of the disease. They were weak after the long journey north from Mexico, which took two stormy months at sea. The two ships were only a small part of an expedition that aimed to settle California by land and water; the *San Antonio* had left Baja one month later than the others. They had not expected to arrive first, but when they reached San Diego harbor, only sand and seagulls greeted them. Alarmed Diegueño Indians on the beach ran away. The native people feared the tall white ship, which they first thought was a giant whale. The *San Antonio* was the first Spanish vessel to anchor in Alta California in 166 years.

Morale on the eighty-foot sailboat had improved only at the prospect of meeting up with the *San Carlos,* which had gone ahead. But here it was, in such sad condition. All the way north the ship had fought fog and wind. Though its captain, Vicenta Vila, had turned out to sea to avoid being grounded, the weather had not improved. Blown off course in the wide ocean, the ship wandered, lost. One hundred days after it left Mexico, the *San Carlos* had reached the climax of its bad luck. Its sailors weakened, one by one.

The horror of scurvy dealt a hard blow to all the Spanish sailors' hopes. San Diego's blue spring skies and perfect weather seemed to mock them. Those who were able wrestled the ill to shore and set up a tent camp, where the desert conditions and wary Diegueño people offered no quick remedy. Ship doctor Pedro Prat found as many green herbs and berries as he could, feeding them in stews and teas to the dying sailors as the body count climbed. In all, scurvy claimed thirty-four men, more than a third of the two crews. From sailcloth shelters, the survivors feebly greeted the land expedition when it arrived at last, a full month later.

More sailors perished from scurvy than from all other sicknesses, storms, or battles worldwide. Not until 1795 did the nautical world learn that the disease could be prevented by eating fresh vegetables and citrus. The crews of the *San Antonio* and *San Carlos* might have been saved by oranges and lemons, produce that, ironically, would make Southern California famous in years to come.

1781

An Offer They Couldn't Refuse

The plaza was full of people, despite the midday heat. As Captain Fernando Rivera y Moncada spoke to the residents of western New Spain, he dabbed sweat from his forehead and boasted of the glories of their new northern territory, Alta California. He had just come from there, and had observed with his own eyes a pleasant climate and a growing chain of missions. He had met with California's governor, Felipe de Neve, and conveyed from him a generous offer: twenty-four families would be paid to settle near the Rio de Porciúncula, a small river close to the Mission San Gabriel. "Stay and listen," Rivera told those gathered around him, "to hear news of a better life!"

He made the offer to all who would listen. Each settler willing to go north to the California frontier would receive ten pesos a month, plus clothing, tools, and enough rations to survive until the first crops matured. Each would be provided with materials for building a home and land for farming and grazing. Entire families were invited—especially daughters and sisters of marriageable age, who surely would find husbands among the region's many eligible soldiers.

The Spanish governors thought they offered a good deal. But the longer Rivera spoke, the fewer the people who stayed to hear him. The hot weather was not the only problem—people just weren't interested.

Why was the army captain having such trouble finding any takers? Rivera had marched through all of Sonora looking for settlers to go north. He had been stuck under orders; he could not move on to other business until he had filled his roster. But few people would hear him out, least of all those who were the sort the frontier region wanted.

From the presidio in the California capital of Monterey, Governor Felipe de Neve had been very specific about the kind of settlers he desired for the new southern California town. The head or father of each family must be a man of the soil, and married. He should be healthy, robust, and without known vices or defects—he must impress the local Gabieliño Indians and not take advantage of them. Needed most were a carpenter to build yokes and solid wooden *carretas,* or carts, and a blacksmith to make plows, pickaxes, and crowbars. The recruits must be willing to commit to ten years in the new town, and should be prepared for "the hardships of the frontier."

This final requirement may have been the problem. Rivera's promises of free land and livestock could not blind the people of northern Mexico to what they knew: their remoteness from the capitals of New Spain meant they were easily ignored by Spanish politics. Alta California was a nowhere land for those who hoped to improve their rank and status. People of pure Spanish blood found better opportunities in civilized areas or, at the worst, in the military post at Monterey, many days' travel north of the proposed pueblo.

For another thing, the terms weren't as generous as they sounded. Government pay in New Spain was irregular at best. Rations came on a varied schedule, too. Creating a town from scratch was hard work: within one year the settlers had to build houses and canals and pitch in on the construction of government presidios at whatever rate the army specified. Each male had militia responsibilities during emergencies, and all would be watched closely for five years. Even then their land was not entirely free and clear—neither it nor the houses could ever be sold. Was it really any wonder that, after three months, Rivera had found no one willing to go north?

The governor would not let him off the hook, however. California needed farmers to help discourage curious explorers from England and Russia. So all through the hot summer Rivera talked of golden opportunities, and by August he had found seven settlers with the necessary virtues. Eventually, a few more suitable families joined them.

For these *vecinos pobladores,* or poor country folk, the offer that so many others had turned down was one they couldn't refuse. In a rigid culture where skin color determined prestige, the eleven families who headed north on foot had little influence. Only two men were of "white" Spanish blood. The rest of the forty-four settlers were black, creole, mestizo, mulatto, or Native American. All were poor enough to take a chance and brave enough to make it work. They had nothing to lose.

In 1781, the little band of settlers and livestock moved up the California coast. The oldest settler was Basilio Rosas, 67 years old, who traveled with his wife and six children. After seven months of walking, he and the others reached their land of promise, and on high ground near the gravel bed of a slow-flowing river, they outlined a plaza measuring 200 by 300 feet. Officially founded on September 4, 1781, this little place became a center of opportunity—a small, multiracial frontier town named for Nuestra Señora La Reina de los Angeles del Rio de Porciúncula, the Queen of the Angels. Today we abbreviate that cumbersome name; we simply call it Los Angeles, or L.A.

1835

Dana's Rappel

From the top of the high bluff, the captain sent for the ship's longest ropes. He then gave his command: someone must volunteer to dangle over the side of the cliff and hang there, four hundred feet above the ocean.

At the land's edge, the ship's crew could look down and see their shipmates far below them, tiny as mice. Beyond only a few feet of sand, their own brig, the *Pilgrim*, bounced and bobbed as seawater spouted from the rocks. None of the men who stood at the edge of the bluff wanted to do what their captain had ordered—drop over the side just to retrieve a few measly cattle hides.

The older men said the youngest boys, who were light and active, ought to be the ones to drop. The boys said the opposite, that strength and experience were necessary. All agreed that the high land near Mission San Juan Capistrano was a perfect place for cliff swallows, not sailors.

Only one of the crew had stood on that spot before—and it was he who did what no one else would even consider. Richard Henry Dana was neither the oldest nor youngest man there. He later wrote in his journal what happened next.

"We found a stake fastened strongly into the ground, and apparently capable of holding my weight, to which we made one end of the halyards well fast, and taking the coil . . . threw it over the brink," he said. He wore nothing but the coarse linen shirt, tough trousers, and hat of a typical New England sailor, the "common sea-rig" of warm weather travel. "I began my descent, by taking hold of the rope in each hand, and slipping down, sometimes breasting off with one hand and foot against the precipice, and holding on to the rope with the other." The cliffs were soft, sandy, and might easily have given way.

Dana carefully worked his way down the woven lifeline until he came to a shelf in the rock and sand. On this, he saw the hides that had gotten stuck on their way down to the beach. Holding the rope all the while, he scrambled into the cleft and pulled the hides free, tossing them to the winds with the help of gravity.

Six months earlier, Dana had tossed his first cattle hide from the grand viewpoint where his shipmates waited. He was not yet used to the work. Only twenty years old, Dana was from Boston, Massachusetts—from Harvard, to be exact. College study has made his eyes weak, so he had signed onto the *Pilgrim* as a common sailor, hoping to see the world better than the pages he read. Dana was not as hardened as his shipmates, but neither was he a weakling. Fresh air and sea travel had given him grit.

Collecting hides along the California Coast was a rough trade. These men, sailors for the American company of Bryant & Sturgis, had been hired to fill their ship's hull with tanned hides that would sell for two dollars each to the leather factors and shoemakers of Boston. To obtain the hides, they bartered a cargo of manufactured goods to the Californios, ranchers who used hides like bank notes to buy luxury items—silk, sugar, or cigars—that they could not make themselves. The well-dressed dons had plenty of cattle hides to trade. Their ranchos were huge tracts of land, on which grazed equally large herds. They also had all the cattle from the old Spanish missions. It had been only one year since the Mexican government had divided the mission holdings, and the ranchos had gotten most of the spoils.

Moving the bulky cattle hides aboard ship was difficult labor. Dried flat in the sun, each was folded into an awkward square, hair side in, then loaded onto mules or carts and piled on the beach. The men lifted the folded hides up and balanced them on their heads, and waded barefoot out to a small boat anchored just offshore. The sailors repeated the process at site after site along the coast, until enough hides were stowed away to pay for their ship's journey home. Men who had gotten used to "tossing a hide" could load hundreds in a short time and had earned the right to be considered tough.

Loading hides from San Juan Capistrano was even more difficult, since the mission was perched high above the sandy beach on which the men had landed. A narrow trail led to the top of the cliffs, but the best method of getting hides down relied on gravity: the men flung the hides off the brink like so many pieces of wood. Trouble was, the large, flat squares didn't always drop in a straight line. Caught by ocean breezes this time, more than a dozen fell against the massive cliff and lodged in its nooks and crannies. No one reaching from the top could move them.

Dana had one thing his shipmates did not—a sense of adventure. He volunteered to make the drop by rope. He reached the bottom safely, but his grand rappel got no extra credit from his peers. They all agreed he'd been a "damned fool" to risk his life for skins worth twenty dollars. But the episode served him well when he wrote his book about the California hide trade, *Two Years Before the Mast,* published in 1840. And the bluff that Dana dropped over still bears his name. Today it's called Dana Point.

1846

The Old Woman's Gun

A fter only a few bursts of gunshot, the American soldiers knew in their hearts that they were surrounded. Hunkered down in thorny coastal scrub and mustard plants that grew higher than their heads, the men could hear the clatter of horses and the noise of troops. They could not see their attackers, but with each crashing shot dust rose on all sides.

The American soldiers, led by William Mervine, had landed at San Pedro harbor and were marching northeast to take over the town of Los Angeles from its residents, the Californios. Just as they stopped for a brief rest, the booms of cannon fire surprised them. Hot autumn air closed in on the soldiers as they dropped to the ground and tried to get a clear shot at their enemies. But grapeshot rained down chaotically. Another report echoed—then one more, from the opposite direction. After four of their peers had dropped dead and six more had been wounded by the cannon fire, the Americans turned and ran back to their ships. The battle was over before they could even count the vast number of the troops that had routed them.

The Californios were glad of their opponents' limited view. They had relied upon it. José Antonio Carillo had gathered sixty men from Los Angeles and nearby ranchos, all excellent riders, to fight the American forces as they tried to take the town. The tiny Californio army had one great disadvantage: it had no real weapons. Americans had confiscated the town's guns and ammunition a few months before. All that was left was some gunpowder, borrowed from the Mission San Gabriel, and one rusty gun that had been buried in an elderly woman's yard—a little four-pound cannon that had once been used in the town plaza for firing salutes on festive occasions.

When Carillo and the others realized that Mervine and his men were coming back to fight, the old woman dug up her treasured weapon. The gun had broken off its original mounting, but the Californios tied it on the front axle of a cart to make it mobile. Carillo told the best *caballeros* to hitch their horses to the little cannon on wheels and get ready to ride hard.

Once the Americans took cover in the head-high brush, the Los Angelenos charged. The horsemen circled the American troops, who could not see them. After firing a shot from one side, they turned the cannon sharply and ran it around to the other to fire again. Since Mervine's soldiers could not count their attackers, they had no idea how many guns they faced. Holding willow-branch spears high, Carillo's forces shouted loudly as the random, furious shots scattered the Americans. Several dozen horsemen with just one cannon triumphed against more than three hundred American foot soldiers. The whole town celebrated with the winning defenders.

The old woman had hidden the gun in her yard when the Americans first began to assert their power in what was then Mexican California. The Californios always had been governed from afar and could not see their way of life changing much. They believed that the transformation from one rule to another would be peaceful, even after the American commander Commodore Robert Stockton ("Gassy Bob," as some called him) refused to adapt to the way things were done in California.

Californios, living in the Spanish tradition, slept after lunch and met friends for dinner late at night. The Americans were used to New England time—with a factory-like business day of regular hours—and the newcomers hurled insults at the local men in their colorful velvet serapes and the women in their silk dresses. They called them "thriftless" and "lazy," not understanding that the Californios operated under a different sense of time. Besides, the Californios had wealth to spare. They lived off huge land grants and giant herds of cattle, sheep, and goats. They would have worked harder had it been necessary, but they had no reason to do so. California was a land of plenty.

Commodore Stockton's American representative treated the people of Los Angeles with disrespect. He arrested heads of families for no reason, and even imposed a curfew on the town's residents, sending them home by ten o'clock each night. In bed by ten o'clock? The people of Los Angeles could not imagine it.

Ranchers who called themselves *el gente de razon,* the people of reason, refused to watch their independence die with their social ways. When the situation at last became unpleasant, they determined to rebel. After two months of being treated like children, in politics and in society, they ran the Yankee soldiers out of town.

Strategy and Spanish bravado had won what came to be known as the Battle of the Old Woman's Gun. It was a satisfying success but only a temporary one. Within six months, Stockton's troops retook the city. Though the Calfornios surrendered under easy terms, change was on the horizon. The Americans were here to stay, and the romance of early Southern California would live on only in the stories of dashing riders and one particularly amazing victory.

1849

Christmas in
Death Valley

On Christmas Eve, Juliet Brier and her three sons trudged in the darkness across a dry creekbed. Their feet sunk in the sand now and then, up to their shoe tops in marshy places, but they had come too far to do anything but press onward. Since early fall, they had taken paths no one had traveled before and few have traveled since.

The Reverend John Brier and his wife had come west to find a better life. Their sons, Columbus, John, and Kirk, ages nine, six, and three, had come too, and had walked most of the way across the Great American Desert. The Brier family and the few young men who traveled with them had signed on with the Sand Walking Company, which was headed for California. They had prepared well and had started out driving a sizable herd of cattle alongside their stocked wagons.

But they had not thought that the trek could last so long. They had even taken a "shortcut" east and south of the snowy Sierra Nevada. Unfortunately, the new route crossed the most barren country they'd ever seen.

It was late in December when the little family reached the Valley of Death itself. The landscape shone white and flat, hot and empty. The Briers searched for any sign of water or shade. Mr. Brier scouted ahead with the wagon, and Juliet was left with the three boys and the cattle. Crossing the bottom edge of the mountains was the hardest. "I was sick and weary and the hope of a good camping place was all that kept me up," Mrs. Brier later remembered. The youngest child, Kirk, tired quickly and his mother carried him on her back, barely able to look up under the weight and watch what was ahead.

Together she and the elder boys stumbled across floodplains and ravines to a fire ring where they found the Reverend waiting for them. "Is this the camp?" Mrs. Brier asked.

"No," her husband replied. "It's six miles farther."

It was three o'clock on Christmas morning when the family reached its resting place at a set of flowing springs. The boys could hardly stay awake in the light of the welcome fire. Only in their worst dreams did they reflect that the trail had brought them to the most forbidding place in the world.

At the springs, no one was celebrating the holiday; not one person had energy for music or singing. "We were too far gone for that," Juliet wrote. "The men killed an ox and we had a Christmas dinner of fresh meat, black coffee, and a little bread. I had one small biscuit. You see, we were short on rations then, and didn't know how long we would have to make provisions last."

The only woman in the bunch, Juliet tried to comfort her small boys and the others who gazed silently into the night. Before morning broke, the men asked the Reverend Brier to speak to them—to remind them of home and make them glad they were alive. It was then that one of the young men, Fred Carr, made a kindly suggestion: perhaps Mrs. Brier and her boys should stay at the springs and wait for help, or at least for a guide out of the endless Mojave Desert.

The tired mother was horrified at the suggestion. "Absolutely not!" she protested. Her family had come this far together. And who knew how far the mining camps of California were, anyway? It might be weeks, or even months, before a search party could come back for her. To stop now would mean heat, thirst, hunger, loneliness, and probably a shallow grave.

Christmas morning dawned, showing the group the terrain they had reached: a 150-mile stretch of dry playa filled with salt. The view prompted a decision. The Briers would leave their wagons at the springs near Furnace Creek and pack what they could on the oxen and their own backs. The wagons got bogged down in the clay mud, anyway, and the goods carried in them, including Mrs. Brier's best silver, were of no use to the family now. The party continued westward on foot.

The Briers' decision saved their lives. After two days of walking, they met up with the Jayhawkers, a group of young men who had also burned their wagons and packed what they could carry. They planned to walk over the Panamint Mountains to whatever lay beyond them. The Briers joined the Jayhawkers, and after another numbing month the group came to the first sign of civilization: herds of cattle and new green meadows at the San Francisquito Ranch. It was there, on February 5, that one of the men put down in his journal, "We have got out of trouble at last."

Mrs. Brier and her family had lost all their possessions but they had kept their lives as they crossed Southern California's—and the West's—most forbidding landscape.

1853

The Lone Woman of San Nicolas Island

The small band of Native Americans had lived on the island for as long as they could remember, and the few visits by missionaries or Russian otter hunters had not disturbed their way of life. But the boat with white sails changed everything. Along with stories of towns and missions, it brought one important piece of news: the Mexican government had decided to move the people of San Nicolas Island to the mainland. The ship's crew had come to take them away.

The boat was ready to launch when one of the young brown-haired women looked around for her baby. Where was her daughter? Among the faces that looked back at her, the child's was missing. The woman went ashore to search the village and the beach, but the ship did not wait. With the first wind, it sailed away with all her people.

The woman never found her child; she was left alone. At first she expected that her relatives would come back in another ship to take her, too. Her people were good sea travelers and had made the sixty-mile crossing to the mainland a few times in long plank canoes coated with tar and decorated with bits of shell. It took fourteen men on each side to paddle such boats, and one to bail water constantly. After weeks with no sign of help, the woman realized she had been forgotten. She wandered the island for days, eating no food and drinking nothing but water. Sometimes she stayed up all night, hoping to die. Her clothes tore and her legs bled. The dogs of her former village followed her.

After a very long time she forgot to mourn and began to eat again. There was no reason to stop living. The island was rich with food—plants and nesting colonies of birds and seals that could be snared as they slept on the rocks. Preserving what meat and fish she could catch, she set up camp near the best source of fresh water. Above this spring, she wove baskets which she coated with tar so that they could carry water. Here, too, she sewed clothes made from the skins of birds. From shell and bone she shaped fishhooks and needles. And she watched tall schooners pass in the distance, never stopping.

In the summer of her fiftieth year—seventeen years after the boat had left her alone—the woman watched a ship anchor just offshore. Two pale men and two dark ones landed a smaller boat on the beach and began gathering gull's eggs. She watched from a distance, uncertain of them, as they traveled halfway up the island then left after the clouds began to whisper. It was the first sign that the woman might someday meet her people again. She decided she would go to greet the next boat that came.

Another year passed. Then, in 1853, one of the men, an American named George Nidever, came back to the island. His crew climbed up from the spring to where the woman worked and waited. Her dogs barked at the intruders, but she sent the dogs away. She greeted the men with smiles and indicated with sign language how glad she was to see them. They did not understand her language, but they sat down when she asked them to and ate the baked roots she had prepared.

Nidever sat with the others in a circle around her. It was he who first suggested they go off the island together—that the woman should pack her things and sail away with them. As soon as she understood what he meant, she moved fast and with glee. She stepped to the prow of the small boat that ferried her to the sailing ship and talked to the sailors as it moved, letting out all her years of silence in one great gush. They smiled back at her mysterious words and gave her woven clothes to wear: a striped petticoat, a man's shirt, and a black necktie. All the men agreed that the woman's face was pleasing, even though her teeth were worn to the gums from eating dried seal blubber.

When the men reached their home port of Santa Barbara, the news flashed through the hills like fire: a woman had been left behind on one of the Channel Islands! A crowd assembled. As the woman passed among them, she clapped her hands and laughed at each thing she'd never seen before—a horse, an ox-cart. She settled at the Nidever home, and everyone in town came to see her and her dresses, baskets, and things from the island. Some brought presents; others wanted to take her north, to the city, and exhibit her in public. This last thing the Nidever family refused. They decided she would live with them.

The woman was always in good humor and often sang her people's songs. But no one alive could understand her words. The padres from the nearby Mission Santa Barbara sent for Indians from different parts of the coast, hoping that one day the woman could tell the story of her life alone on the island. None of the visitors spoke the same dialect that she did. On the entire coast, she was the last of her tribe. By means of signs and pantomime, she communicated the above story. It is all we know of her life.

A month after she was brought to Santa Barbara, the woman became sick. Her solitary life had left her vulnerable to the American town's diseases. Seven weeks from the day of her arrival, she died. The priests at the mission buried her within the shady, walled grounds.

The lone woman of San Nicolas Island had seen the new California. A shadow of its isolated past, she had disappeared twice—once, with her own people, and another time in the quick pace and turmoil of the new era. She was a symbol of California's rapidly changing, sometimes tragic human history.

1871

An Atmosphere of Suspicion

Kuang Kao and Heng Huo wanted to get married. The young lovers had come to America from China. They owed the cost of their passage to separate *tongs,* organizations that had brought them across the Pacific Ocean. The problem was that the two young Chinese owed loyalty to rival tongs, each of which guarded its turf ferociously. Though the pair swore they were in love, their sponsoring groups would hear of no such union.

The two immigrants had begun their romance on the crowded streets of Chinatown in Los Angeles, where posters lettered in inky characters proclaimed goods for sale. Chinatown extended along both sides of Alameda Street and housed more people per square foot than any other part of the city. The English- and Spanish-speaking citizens of Los

Angeles had little to do with the Chinese quarter, visiting it only if they wanted exotic goods: green tea, embroidered shawls and handkerchiefs, candied ginger, even opium. Left mostly to themselves, the Chinese lived by the rules of the two tongs that governed the area.

Kuang Kao and her new lover had tried to escape from those who claimed to own them by running away to Santa Barbara. But the leaders of Chinatown would not be denied. They determined to bring the pair back and to use the American legal system to do it. The bosses told the police that Kuang Kao was a notorious criminal. They were on hand to mock her when she stepped from the train at San Pedro in custody. Eventually, the charges against Kuang Kao were dropped.

Then Heng Huo planned an even better ruse. Why not get married the American way, enlisting the double forces of law and church on their side? In a small chapel, Kuang Kao became Heng Huo's wife and a member of his clan. That night, Chinatown exploded. Shots burst from open windows, fireworks exploded at all hours, and angry voices argued in the alleys. The Chinese tongs fussed and boiled. No one was injured, but the air throbbed with the noise of ire and celebration.

Just outside the Chinese section, the residents of greater Los Angeles fidgeted. Something was going on in Chinatown; signs of vice were more pronounced than usual. The police, already tired of the section's intrigues, chafed at the sounds of pistol fire. Even if they had known the lovers' story, the Angelenos would not have been inclined toward sympathy. Most thought all Chinese were immoral and not entitled to the protection of the law.

The codes of the Chinese tongs were indecipherable to mainstream Los Angeles, and its residents did not want to understand them. The language barrier made it hard for the small number of Chinese workers to blend into the larger population. Most non-Asian people thought that the Chinese made few efforts to become culturally American. The courts wouldn't have allowed them full legal rights anyway. In the "Yellow Peril" legislation of the time, Chinese were excluded from U.S. citizenship.

In this atmosphere of suspicion, something unexpected happened. On the night of October 24, 1871, police entered the Chinese quarter to break up an argument between members of the tongs. By whim or by accident, someone in the Chinese section killed a white policeman. Shots were fired, and one hit officer Robert Thompson. Fellow officers carried him to a nearby drugstore, where he died. The policemen responded to the murder of one of their own with something worse than murder: organized vigilante action. Mobs of non-Asian men grabbed guns and ropes and descended on the now quiet Chinese streets. In the next five grisly hours, they killed as many Chinese men as they could catch, dragging some down the street by their braided hair or with a noose. A Chinese doctor was killed for the money in his pockets and the diamond ring on his finger. In all, the mob stole $40,000 from Chinatown homes and businesses. The next morning, nineteen bodied lay in a row near the jail. At most, only one of the dead men could have been accused of any wrongdoing.

Some said the war in Chinatown was started by love, but others knew it for what it was: a battle over race and money.

Despite that violent night, the Chinese continued to prosper. Even in the 1870s, when the California gold rush era was fizzling out to nothing, the Chinese made strides toward wealth. They fished for abalone and sold the meat to China as a delicacy; within a few years this became a million-dollar industry. The immigrants also raised vegetables, ran laundries, and worked many jobs, some in Angeleno households as domestic servants. They grew a merchant class, and their trade networks spread. Today, Chinese and other Asian immigrants and their descendants make up one of the fastest-growing sectors of California's population.

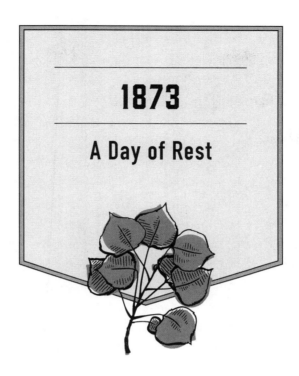

1873

A Day of Rest

The hired cook broke the seal on the oven door and lifted an aromatic stew from the still-hot coals. As she set the steaming dish before him, Joseph Newmark thought how each Saturday the warm midday meal seemed like a minor miracle: it had simmered in the cast-iron stove for nearly twenty-four hours, untouched by flame or human hands. Newmark enforced Jewish Sabbath law in his household and said no one could perform work from Friday night until Saturday at sunset. "This will be the best *chamim* yet," Newmark pronounced from his seat at the head of the table. "Already I can taste the garlic and sweet California onions."

With a prayer of thanks, Newmark broke one of two loaves of sweet white challah bread for his guests at this most important Sabbath luncheon. The twelve friends and family members ate the spicy stew of chickpeas and beef, sopping up the best juices with the bread, in recognition of the importance of ritual. Here in the far West, they were keeping the same traditions that their forefathers had kept for thousands of years. As God himself had commanded Moses, they were reserving the seventh day of the week for rest and celebration.

For Jewish people throughout the world, every Saturday was a holy day. But this week in Los Angeles, the Sabbath luncheon was even more important: Congregation B'nai B'rith was celebrating a sign of permanence. After twenty years of growth, the small Jewish community had built its first tall, stately synagogue. Those who feasted at Newmark's table had just come from the new temple on Fort Street.

Lifting glasses of brandy, the men toasted progress made manifest in the new solid brick building. It signified stability, with leaded glass windows and heavy wooden doors. Within the new building, they and their families had assembled, men on the main floor and women in the balcony, to give thanks. They had come together this day like ingredients for the Sabbath stew, with an equally happy result.

Over his dinner, Newmark remembered less cohesive times. Like other restless young men, he had come west in 1854, intending to raise his fortune by selling supplies to miners in the gold rush. Selling goods came naturally to many of the young Jewish pioneers, since their ancestors had also worked in the "backpack business," trading whatever goods they could carry. Spices, furs, fabrics, precious stones—these things became their treasure when persecution in Europe drove them from place to place.

But the American frontier was not organized around the young men's religion. For instance, because kosher butchers were rare, they had to learn to prepare their own food according to dietary law. They worked Saturdays, in spite of their faith, since the adobe shops of Los Angeles stayed open. They met for worship when their work allowed, in private homes or rented spaces. Even when they could not obey all the laws of their religion, Newmark and his peers had kept the Sabbath by gathering on Friday nights to light candles and bless their shared wine.

Just this year, the Jewish men had helped found the new Chamber of Commerce, and they had been called the city's "best citizens" in the local newspaper. Together with their wives and children, they formed a Hebrew Benevolent Society and purchased lots for a Jewish cemetery. As Newmark himself was proud of noting, they shared a sense of upward mobility and a willingness to adapt.

The Jewish men and women of the City of Angels shared something else: a particularly American brand of freedom. In frontier Los Angeles, Jewish people were allowed to thrive as they seldom had in eastern or European cities. The "Israelites," as non-Jews called them, found a remarkable atmosphere of tolerance in Southern California. Unlike the Chinese, who looked so obviously different, they were not persecuted as they had been in so many places, for so many centuries. Living side by side with Catholics and Methodists, they entered the worlds of business and government. Their names could be found on the pages of the local Blue Book—a guide to the booming town—and on the membership rosters of local societies.

Now, with the completion of the Fort Street synagogue, they had made their mark on the land, too. The building was a solid, beautiful symbol of their hopes for the future.

Newmark and the men at his table spoke of the temple's beauty as they basked in this day of rest. It had taken them twenty years of enterprise and hard work to build a place where they could worship. Like God, who rested on the seventh day, they felt the satisfaction of having been present at the creation.

Just after sunset at the Havdalah ceremony that ended the Sabbath day, Joseph Newmark started his new week. It was a gentle August evening. In an atmosphere rich with wine, spices, and the yellow, flickering light from a candle, the patriarch of the Los Angeles Jewish community may have imagined that California would grow once trains reached it from the East. He may have pictured the arrival of more German and, later, Russian Jews to swell his congregation's ranks. In the room's darkest shadows he may have foreseen the horrible World Wars that would bring even more of his people west. But in his best dreams he could not have imagined what would one day come to pass: that Los Angeles would hold more than 150 Jewish congregations, and that by the mid-twentieth century it would be home to more Jews than anywhere in the world outside Israel and New York City.

1888

Letting in the Sunshine

Sunny Southern California can stop the effects of old age!" the promotional pamphlets cried. The extravagant promise found eager readers. In an age of tuberculosis, dry coughs and aching joints weighed on the minds of many. But health seekers had found their golden land in the sea breezes of the Pacific Coast. Southern California was a pleasant place of palm trees and gentle waves, of sun and constant seventy-degree weather.

Word got out fast that California's climate could cure anything. One booklet produced by the railroad said that people who lived near the western ocean had fewer enlarged glands and liver problems, and fewer cases of chronic pneumonia, malaria, or jaundice. Taking the waters at a desert spa heightened the curative effect: it relieved constipation, skin disease, and insomnia. From sooty, smoky Boston and Chicago, the tourists came, saw, and settled. Thousands—fifty thousand in 1885 alone, and double that number two years later—poured into the land of flowers and sunshine.

The locals looked on all this movement with a skeptical eye. After all, they'd had a few bouts with sickness in their lives. Common colds and the usual diseases ran rampant in season, even in the sunny Southland. Besides, the dusty streets, coastal fogs, damp earthen houses, and wood smoke of the region's towns hardly seemed the thing to cure lung disease. Newspaper editors worried that the new citizens, confined to their sickbeds, would not help the area's population in the long run. But the people kept coming, lured by promises and cheap rail tickets. Every town's population swelled. With four to six times the number of residents they'd had in the past, communities now found their public services were stretched to the max.

Real estate prices shot up in Los Angeles, where city lots cost ten times what they had the year before. Gullible newcomers bought eroding beach property or desert orchards, sight unseen. They took rooms in crowded boardinghouses with no light or air just to be part of the trend. Faith-healers swooped down on those willing to listen, and morticians— who swept in on those whom faith-healing failed—had the run of their lives.

Developers loved the inrush; it was only natural that they wished to exploit it. Their best idea tapped the funds of wealthy tourists and newcomers who wanted rooms with a view. Builders made palaces for all who could afford them. In Pasadena, Riverside, and other communities linked to the Southern Pacific Railway, they set up the scaffolding for grand tourist hotels—perfect for invalids who wished to recover in style.

The king of all these grand clinics was the Hotel del Coronado, built on a sandbar near San Diego by two Midwesterners who saw climate as a commodity. E. S. Babcock and H. L. Story bought land on what was then known as the San Diego Peninsula. They renamed the place Coronado Island, playing up associations with the tropics. After dividing the land's long beaches into house lots, they built a hotel that was an invalid's dream. Each room had a view of the water and a porch or patio to let in the sunshine. Once the hotel's curving central walls were up, its builders added stage setting from the jungle—sea turtles to walk its lawns and cage full of swinging monkeys. On Coronado Beach, visitors could feel summer even in February, the month the Queen Anne–style hotel opened. "Airy, picturesque, half-bizarre," as Edmund Wilson wrote, the Hotel del Coronado topped them all.

The health rush proved that California was the Golden State. Though it did not quite live up to all its claims, America's Mediterranean was not too much of a disappointment. Year-round flowers, daily sunshine, and breezy hotel rooms made it an easy place to spend the rest of a sickly life.

1891

So Much Depends on a Bug

The orange growers near Riverside watched as the small, red bugs crawled from a wooden packing box and flew into the trees. The round Australian beetles with black spots were the growers' best hope in hard times. Smoke, fogs, and pesticides had not been able to stop the spreading blight that was ruining the area's juicy citrus crops. The growers had imported these small insects, known as ladybugs, to save their groves.

With the help of irrigation, the hillsides south of the San Bernardino Mountains had become the center of the young citrus industry. Though Spanish missionaries had planted many varieties of orange trees in their compounds, the Washington navel orange—a sweet, seedless variety from Brazil—had become the favorite crop. By the 1880s, California farmers sent navel oranges and summer Valencias to the entire nation by railroad refrigerator cars.

The granite soil in the state's citrus belt made for healthy seedlings with dark green leaves. Warm air rose from the valley bottoms, and the water carried all the right nutrients from the soil to the seedlings. Farmers in Ontario, Redlands, and surrounding towns planted rows of young orange trees and protected them by planting more trees—cypress windbreaks. Fairs and festivals flourished in the area, celebrating the white blossoms of the golden crop.

Then, in the late 1880s, the clear skies clouded over. One of the growers checked the ripening oranges on his trees and found a damaged crop. The skin of the round fruit had thinned in places and was dry like cotton. Tiny, nearly invisible bugs were eating the rind and injecting it with decay. Cushion scale, the growers called it. It spread from grove to grove, ruining harvests. The disease had probably come from Australia or South America on new orange varieties or seedlings. In California, there was nothing to slow its progress. The scab-like growths resisted everything the growers threw at them. Even using the latest technology, the farmers could not get rid of the pests.

Just when it looked like the orange crop was doomed, the United States Department of Agriculture sent a special investigator to Australia to study cottony cushion scale firsthand. The investigator came back with a small packet that he hoped would solve everything. In it were ladybird beetles, the scale's natural enemy.

Could a small bug save the orange crop? It seemed unlikely. But the friendly ladybugs could and did. They cleaned out the scale in record time, stopped the spread of blight, and became tiny superheroes.

In 1891, more than two thousand railcars left from California citrus belt sidings. Five million orange trees made the Southland fragrant. Today more oranges are grown in Florida, or in Brazil, but the ladybug's legacy remains visible to those who visit California by car. At the state border, members of the agricultural patrol check all fruit for blight or bugs before harvest time. The little polka-dotted beetle saved an industry that remains vigilant today.

1900

Leaving Independence

From the back door of her little brown house at the edge of town, Mary Hunter Austin watched the sun sink behind Mount Kearsarge. Gradually, the mountain turned black and tentlike in silhouette. The small woman felt an ache in her heart, a feeling of loss. In the dimming pink light of the Eastern Sierras, Mary faced the hardest decision of her thirty-one years: whether to leave, or to stay in the land that she loved.

She turned from the door to sit at her writing table, where she tried to put her thoughts on paper. "East away from the Sierras, south from Panamint and Amargosa, east and south many an uncounted mile, is the Country of Lost Borders," she wrote. So began a flood of words that would describe the places she had seen and loved. "There are hills, rounded, blunt, burned, squeezed up out of chaos," she continued, "chrome and vermilion painted, aspiring to the snowline."

Mary Austin had the innate urge to write about desert places that no one else recognized as valuable. She wrote of the "intolerable sun glare" and the way rainfall gathered in the hollows of the hills. She saw life and death in every scene, and no wonder: her own life had been filled with heartache and loss.

That night in the little town of Independence, California, as the sky's hue darkened from rosy orange to midnight blue, Mary sat at her desk and wrote what she knew. She told of the playas and mesquite flats around her little hometown, and of the sheepherders and tough bristlecone pines that survived there. She wrote of her own little house beneath a willow tree, and of Paiute and Shoshone Indians who lived along the foothills. Mary wrote until her hand cramped. Her writings formed themselves, like clouds, into a welcome collection that, in time, she would call *The Land of Little Rain.*

Mary's stories focused on bravery. They were tales of life among dry hills and scant oases. Mary's life along the Eastern Sierra front, in Owens Valley, had required such courage. She had faced grief and sorrow in the fourteen years that she'd lived there. Her husband, Wallace Austin, had lost everything in a failed irrigation scheme. When the money ran out, he left her alone and pregnant to be evicted from their lodgings. Though he came back after a time, he remained cold and emotionally distant. Marriage was a trial.

So was motherhood. Mary nearly died giving birth to their only daughter, Ruth, who had a beautiful face but a damaged mind. She could not speak or learn as other children could. Though the local Paiute people brought herbs and meadowlark's tongues to try to cure the child, the young mother felt alone in the world. She had nothing to protect her but the long hair she piled atop her head.

To keep her spirits from sinking to the dusty ground, Mary focused on the thing she most admired: the desert land itself. She identified with its hardy plants, the small bits of greenery that thrived in a harsh environment. When Wallace went away for weeks at a time, sometimes without warning, she staved off loneliness by paying attention to the stark, arid countryside. She had found a way to manage.

Mary's love of the desert was what poured from her pen that night. Later, as she dotted her manuscript with the last period of the last sentence and wrapped it in brown paper and string, she knew that she would have to leave Owens Valley to become a writer. If there were readers willing to learn about this country, she wanted to tell its stories. Sharing the desert's "palpable mystery" was the best thing she could offer to others. But she would have to go out into the larger world and force it to listen.

The Land of Little Rain was published a year later and became a success. By that time Mary had already packed her bags onto a wagon and taken Ruth west to the coast, leaving Wallace and the little town of Independence. But she never really left the land where so little moisture falls. She carried the landscape of the Eastern Sierra in her mind wherever she traveled, to Eastern cities or European capitals. As a famous writer who, a hundred years later, still stands as one of the region's best naturalists, she wrote a dozen books about the land that had inspired and consoled her. Her words introduced thousands of readers to the California desert. "For all the toll the desert takes of a man it gives compensations," she announced to the whole world. "Deep breaths, deep sleep, and the communion of the stars."

1905

A Destructive Dream

The settlers in the Imperial Valley had an unerring faith in human ingenuity. Engineering could save them—it could make the desert bloom! Not until the ruddy, raging waters of the Colorado River gushed out of control onto the valley floor did the people of the Imperial Valley realize that man was not God. The giant river had changed its course at flood stage and now threatened to swamp them all. And it had happened because of a colossal human mistake.

The Imperial farmers' dream had been to create an irrigated oasis of a wide, dry mineral valley in southeast California. They had purchased a piece of land known as the Salton Sink, which did resemble a huge basin. More than two hundred feet below sea level, it was a dip in the earth's crust. Real estate companies had renamed the depression the Imperial Valley. With water from the nearby Colorado River, they said, the whole region could be a wealthy agricultural kingdom.

Such dreams did not seem unreasonable. After all, the Sink had been filled with water in fossil times; it had been part of the Sea of Cortez. Silt from the Colorado River had blocked the inlet over time and left in its place a thick, red soil full of nutrients. Wheat and lettuce and melons should grow well in what was now only a salt marsh.

The developers spoke of water with teary, glazed eyes. Water, they said, would solve everything. It was a perennial problem in the dry inland region. Each year the land needed more water than it got from the clouds. Between them, farmers and real estate agents hatched a plan to get the liquid gold they needed: they could redirect the Colorado's generous flow. Human technology could help them tap the mighty river that was only a short distance away. The red river drained seven states and ran 1,440 miles. It seemed to have water to spare.

Of course, tapping any river took special skills. So the California Development Company brought in an engineer to do the groundwork. George Chaffey was a Canadian who had built canals in other parts of the state, and he knew what was required. After six weeks of research, he designed a canal that curved south through part of Mexico. The water would follow it to an older river channel and then spill back into the Salton Sink. In 1901 the ditch was complete, and the Imperial Valley turned green overnight.

Chaffey had neglected to take one fact into account. The Colorado was a muddy, heavy stream clogged with sediment from its lengthy journey south from the Rocky Mountains.

Whenever its flow was slowed—in an irrigation ditch, for instance—it dropped sand and silt. The mud quickly plugged small channels. By 1904, it had nearly cut off Chaffey's ditch to the Imperial Valley.

The farmers then took matters into their own hands. Though the U.S. Reclamation Service had warned them that the Colorado River was too large to tamper with, they guided their share of water through a new route, a "temporary" ditch south of the Mexican border that again emptied into the old channel and the Salton lows. Easily planned, easily done.

Then came spring. The river roiled, overflowed with mountain snowmelt, and cut through the many layers of silt where its banks were weak. One of the weak spots was the farmer's new ditch. The Colorado broke through and began to empty its entire flow into the Salton basin. A thousand miles of water poured down in a silty, sticky flow that measured nearly 90,000 cubic feet of water per second. No hand-dug ditch could hold back that kind of power.

The water poured into the salty basin for two years. It cost the Southern Pacific Railway three million dollars, wages for two thousand Indian laborers, and three thousand train cars of rock to turn the river back to where it had originally flowed. Thousands of acres of farmland in the higher parts of the valley were saved, but thousands more now sat at the bottom of an inland sea that had no outlet. The trapped water grew more salty with each month, as its minerals concentrated through evaporation. The new salty lake was fifty miles long, fifteen miles wide, and forty feet deep.

The farmers who still had dry land to plow praised the massive rescue team, saying it had proved human brainpower could tame the landscape. Those who found their land drowned along with their hopes came away with a different message—don't mess with Mother Nature. Today's Salton Sea, still evaporating, is more than 30 miles long and 15 miles wide. Its water is as salty as any ocean.

1907

Walking on Water

Waves broke midway up the pier in a curling aquamarine cascade. As each billow crashed and ran out in an apron of bright bubbles, the power of the Pacific Ocean became evident. To the spectators on the strand at Redondo Beach, dressed in polished shoes and natty linens, the water held a dangerous beauty. It seemed unlikely that the young man before them, who seemed to walk atop its froth, would survive.

Unlike the people on the beach and pier, the young man was dressed for the sea. His short woolen costume covered him, for modesty, and also kept him warm in ocean water. He paddled his eight-foot board out through the breaks in the waves, then turned and pulled himself up quickly to crouch on the floating board. The crowd chuckled, uneasily. They were certain he could not manage to stay upright in such thunderous surf.

The young man on the wooden board had no doubt about his safety, though. George Freeth was a Hawaiian who had grown up with the Pacific under his skin. Born on the island of Oahu in 1883, he was outwardly a *haole,* a white man, who resembled his Irish grandfather. Freeth's ancestors had sought a better life in the goldfields of California but had gone even farther west to succeed. His mother's family was partly native Hawaiian, so George, like many from the islands, counted an understanding of the ocean in his heritage.

Freeth loved to swim in open water. It was not a popular activity at the time. At Redondo Beach, most tourists frequented the saltwater plunge that developer Henry Huntington had built seaside. Man-made saltwater pools were safer than the riptides beyond the sand. The young man with the carved board had no fear of currents. Paddling over breaking waves, he took his board out to deeper water and waited for the chance to ride the bouncing crest. When his chance came, he did the unthinkable. While catching one of the rolling breakers, he bent down and grasped his board with both hands. He then lifted his feet heavenward. Freeth did a handstand on the crest of a wave! The crowds applauded, having never seen anything like it.

Demonstrating his art at Redondo and at nearby Moonstone Beach, George Freeth was Southern California's first real surfer. He was not the first man to attempt to ride the waves of the California coastline, however. Thirty years before him, a trio of young Hawaiians attending school in San Mateo decided to brave the surf at Santa Cruz. In 1885, the locals were amused by the athleticism of these swimming

Hawaiian "princes" as they rode their homemade redwood boards off the mouth of the San Lorenzo River.

Swimming with boards, an old art, was just dying out in Hawaii itself. Though it once had been known as the sport of native kings, surfing was now limited to a few diehard practitioners. On Waikiki Beach in Hawaii, a relatively small group of young men attempted to revive the art. They called themselves the Hui Nalu Club. Among this little group was George Freeth, the old man of the bunch although he was still in his early twenties. Also there was teenager Duke Paoa Kahanamoku. They experimented with waveriding methods. Freeth was muscular, but he was no match for the huge native Hawaiians, so he cut the traditional sixteen-foot board in half and found it easier to move. His skill at waveriding caught the attention of visitors from the mainland. In 1906, the writer Jack London was among those who admired the surf club members' prowess.

An adventurer himself, London talked his companions into trying the sport. As he struggled with his heavy board, half-drowned, he received a vision of the perfect surfer. "Shaking the water from my eyes as I emerged from one wave and peered ahead to see what the next one looked like, I saw him tearing in on the back of it," he wrote. The young surfer was "standing upright with his board, carelessly poised, a young god bronzed with sunburn." It was Freeth, of course.

Jack London was a famous writer, a Californian, and his piece about "surf-bathing" caught the eye of Henry Huntington. Huntington had bought land for cheap in the oil marshes along the coast south of Los Angeles. He built grand resorts along the strand at Redondo Beach and was in the process of developing the residential community that would bear his name—Huntington Beach. In spite of rail lines that ran directly to the shore from city center, Huntington was finding it difficult to draw crowds southward to his hotels and restaurants. He needed a draw. London's article suggested an excellent one: a man who could walk on water.

Thus, in the spring of 1907, Freeth became the first professional surfer. He had moved to the state that would be his making and his home for the rest of his life.

His skills in the water were not limited to showy display. When Huntington's guests showed a reluctance to get in the sea, fearing their poor swimming abilities, Freeth was the first to suggest a solution: post a number of guards who could swim to rescue those in difficulties. He used a mini surfboard—a rescue paddleboard—to help him keep the novices topside. He also invented a torpedo-shaped can float that such lifeguards could pull behind them. Huntington hired him as lifesaver as well as entertainer, and Freeth taught his crew methods for pulling weak swimmers from riptide currents. These methods are still taught today.

Some of his rescues made front page news. After a Japanese fishing boat foundered off Santa Monica, Freeth saved the men on board. They were grateful enough to name their fish camp in Washington after their savior—Port Freeth it remains on some maps today. For this and other difficult feats, Freeth was awarded the highest civilian medal for bravery, the Congressional Gold Medal. He also won the Carnegie Medal for Bravery and the Gold Medal of the U.S. Life Saving Corps.

A fixture along the coast, Freeth was on hand when the famous Hawaiian surfer Duke Kahanamoku surfed Ocean Beach, San Diego in 1912. Duke was on his way to the Olympics in Stockholm, Sweden, where he would win Olympic gold. He, too, demonstrated the art of surfing, at Santa Monica and Corona del Mar. His gold medal cemented his place as one of California's earliest waveriders, and his friend George Freeth welcomed the new popularity of the sport.

Freeth aspired to be a waterman—the best swimmer, surfer, and water polo player he could be. He lived to surf, but he did not live long. When the influenza epidemic of 1918 spread around the world, California was hit hard. Many of the sailors at San Diego caught the virus, which spread up the coast. The 1918 flu was exceptional in that it did not hit only children and the very old, as most influenza does. Instead, it favored anyone, even people in the prime of life, who might have watery lungs or a tendency to pneumonia. As a surfer and lifeguard, Freeth was constantly drinking the ocean. During a series of rescues during a winter storm at Oceanside, he ingested more than his fair share of salt water. With weakened lungs, he was a perfect host for the virus then rampaging through the region. Though he was only thirty-five years old, it plunged him into illness and unemployment. He never recovered. Freeth died at the age of 35 in April 1919.

The sport that he popularized did not die with him. After such surfers as Duke Kahanamoku and the legendary Tom Blake gave Californians a wider taste of the skills required, surfriding took off. Surfers experimented in the 1940s with new materials to make boards lighter and stronger. Bob Simmons invented the first balsa-and-fiberglass board just in time for the novices who came in droves to the beaches during the 1950s. California surfing arrived as large as a rogue wave, spilling over into the music, movies, and fashions of the nation's popular culture.

For many years, a bronze bust of Freeth in his lifesaving gear stood on the margin of the Redondo Beach Pier. Sometimes surfers placed leis around the statue, in tribute; other times, the salt air was the only thing to take notice of it. Sometime in August 2008, Freeth's statue disappeared. The bronze was probably stolen by thieves seeking scrap metal to melt for cash.

Freeth's bronze god status was not diminished by the theft, however. The father of California surfing is also credited as the father of Irish surfing and a contributor to the profession of life saving in Australia. The film *Waverider* (2009) documents his importance for a new generation of surfers as far away as Glencolmcille, County Donegal, Ireland.

1910

Violent Times

At 1:07 a.m. on October 1, 1910, the headquarters of the Los Angeles *Times* was rocked by a tremendous blast. The explosion set barrels of ink on fire and blew apart the heavy stone walls, crumbling them to shards and blocking any view of the building behind thick black smoke and flame. It did even worse things to the people inside—twenty men working the night shift were killed, and many more lay injured.

"A terrorist bombing!" the *Times* editors cried. The next day's newspaper, just four pages long, blamed the blast on union thugs. The publisher of the paper, Harrison Gray Otis, agreed. A certified union-hater, the former Civil War officer had taken on the battle for free labor as a personal crusade. He had made many pointed comments about unions and their crippling strikes, some of them in print. The blast was surely some kind of revenge. "It's the crime of the century," he said, and he vowed to find out who had done it.

The unionists themselves denied it—they were not responsible, they said, but they were just as angry. Workers had died in the blast. Pointing back in Otis's direction, they blamed him for not maintaining his press facilities. Earlier in the same week, *Times* employees had complained of a gassy smell in the building. Labor now suggested that the stingy Otis had not repaired the gas leak. He had committed murder, by neglect, they charged.

For nearly three years, union activity had worried the residents of Los Angeles. Some said bombs were typical of the fight. With Otis on the warpath, none of the pro-labor forces could afford to back down. They stuck to their beliefs even when police investigators ruled that the tragedy at the newspaper office was indeed the work of terrorism: the blast had been caused by dynamite. Throughout the city, the people of Los Angeles took sides even as they were confused by the issues. And who wouldn't be?

Six months after the bombing, the District Attorney announced he'd found the men who had done it: two unionist brothers from Indianapolis. John J. McNamara was a union secretary, and his brother James worked with him as an organizer. A stool pigeon said that the brothers had blown up the *Times* with a suitcase full of explosives, and he'd seen them do it.

"It's a frame-up!" the unions cried. The turmoil spread, reaching into city politics. With the support of the unions behind him, a local politician ran for mayor as a Socialist. His party was known for its close ties to union workers, and it looked as though he might win. Ten thousand workers marched in the streets in support of the union cause. Otis jeered at them in his weekly newspaper columns.

Labor leaders hired a well-known attorney, Clarence Darrow, to represent the McNamaras. The case went to trial in the middle of 1911, and the entire nation watched. Then, only four days before the city election, just when it looked like Los Angeles would elect a pro-union mayor, a startling thing happened, turning everything around. The McNamara brothers confessed.

Confessed? The Angelenos who had lent their support to labor were dazed and unbelieving. But it was true—Darrow had talked the men into admitting their guilt. The exact details of the agreement were kept secret. It was the only way, the lawyer said, to save his clients' lives. Disgusted with the turn of events, union supporters deserted their candidate, and the Socialists lost all hopes of electing a mayor. Outside the courthouse, pro-labor pins and pamphlets were trampled underfoot.

Some tried to say that the men were innocent, that they'd been bought off to keep the Socialists from power in California. Others said their lives had been threatened, and that the lads confessed as the only way to save themselves. Guilty or not, the McNamara brothers played a part in crippling union efforts in the state for years to come. Historians may never know who blew up the *Times* building, but the brothers' confession blasted away the union cause. For decades, organized labor in Los Angeles was as dead as the twenty men lost in the fire.

1912

A Reel Western

Dust sprayed from the hooves of their ponies as the Sioux riders surged over the ridge. Behind them, the U.S. Cavalry came thundering through the sagebrush. Stormclouds gathered in the distance as bullets and arrows whizzed through the air. It was war on the Plains—the ferocious resistance of a brave people against encroaching settlers. The skies themselves seemed to roll with chords of dismay as the band of Indians circled a camp of covered wagons and chorused their horrible war whoops.

If only the moviegoers could hear them!

From their seats in the nickel theater, members of the audience murmured and gasped at Tom Ince's latest two-reel silent western. Except for the organ music that pulsed an accompaniment to the flickering images, the scene seemed cut out of history. It was the most realistic—the best—movie they had ever seen.

What the crowd didn't know was that the film *War on the Plains* was more than simple illusion. Its realistic Sioux riders were believable in part because they were real Sioux Indians, rounded up compliments of director Thomas Harper Ince, who had found them camped on the beach at Santa Monica. The skilled Indian horsemen and their slick gun maneuvers had come to Southern California as part of a live Wild West show called the Miller Bros. 101 Ranch Circus. Ince put the actors to work doing what they did best. Now they were riding hard and shooting fast in his silent movies.

Pleasing the crowd with silent western dramas was just what Thomas Ince had worked toward his whole life. A New York director who had made one-reel features for the Independent Motion Picture Company, known as IMP, and for another independent company, Kay Bee, Ince had come to the year-round set called California in 1911. Motion picture cameras needed lots of light, and the sunny Southland provided it. Southern California also gave moviemakers a varied, interesting terrain—beaches for pirate scenes, city streets for Keystone Cops comedies, and rocky hills for westerns. Most of the small film companies could not afford to set up elaborate backdrops, so roving bands of cameramen took to the roads of Hollywood and nearby Los Angeles, searching for ideal sets.

On just such a trek, Ince spotted the 101 Ranch crew and realized he had stumbled upon a treasure. With help from the Kay Bee Company, he hired the whole bunch and set up a permanent film village. The Wild West show actors and their tents formed the nucleus of the little "town"—Inceville, they called it. Ince had the cowboys and Indians run through their acts, and he shot the scenes as he made them up. The actors circled wagons, captured pioneer women, and fled from the cavalry.

Western pictures sold well, better than any other kind, and with his new camp of actors Ince could make films by the dozens. Over the next two years, Ince and his studio directors made more than one hundred short films, with titles like *Custer's Last Fight* and stars such as William S. Hart and Tom Mix.

At Inceville, the famous director pioneered a moviemaking institution—the studio. Instead of gathering individual screenwriters, camera operators, producers, and actors for each picture, Ince put all his "talent" together in one compound. He shot movie after movie with the same crew. He hired the Miller Bros. 101 Ranch Circus for an entire season, and put actors under long-term contracts. After a while, he no longer directed every scene himself but supervised other directors and approved the final product—taking credit for the whole thing, of course. From his first office, a canvas tent, he organized the means of production that would rule the film industry for the next fifty years.

After Ince and the Sioux got together, westerns changed for good. The early melodramatic "horse operas" first filmed in the East found new life in the real West, thanks to California's fantastic settings and Ince's demand for authenticity. Ince gave Hollywood the western as an art form, a legacy that has yet to ride off into the sunset.

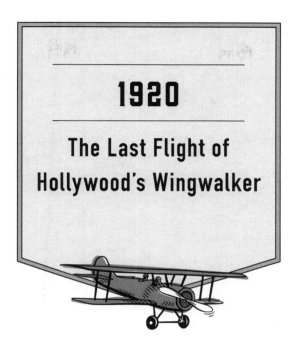

1920

The Last Flight of Hollywood's Wingwalker

The rickety "Jenny" biplane had climbed to 3000 feet in the night sky above Los Angeles and leveled off. The pilot, Ormer Locklear, did some barrel rolls and loops as the bright searchlights illuminated his plane from below, and three cameras on the ground cranked away. In the copilot's seat behind him, his friend "Skeets" Elliott watched "Lock's" deft handling of the light aircraft.

Locklear turned on some of the plane's lights as a signal he was about to start the dive. He flipped a switch and ten magnesium flares burst into life, making the descending plane bright as a meteor as it plummeted to earth. Locklear began to spin as the Jenny fell farther and farther. When the plane was just 500 feet from the ground, some in the crowd felt that something was wrong. It was falling too fast.

Would he be able to pull out in time?

Ormer Locklear had spent his life doing stunts that literally defied death. Luck had always been on his side. He was born October 28, 1891 in the small Texas town of Greenville, not far from Fort Worth. Since his childhood, he had always been enamored of flying, and when America entered "The Great War," Locklear saw a great opportunity. In October 1917, he enlisted in the air service, the fledgling military group that had been hastily formed in an attempt to combat the already powerful German air establishment.

Locklear learned fast and was soon skilled at piloting the Curtiss JN-4 (which was nicknamed the "Jenny"). He was also known for his fearless behavior. Once, when a radiator cap jogged loose from his plane during a training flight, he casually unbuckled his safety belt, climbed out of the cockpit, and, ignoring the hot, stinging water hitting him in the face, replaced the cap and climbed back to his seat.

On another occasion, when a spark plug wire came loose, he climbed out onto the wing and, hanging onto the plane's strut, replaced the wire in midair.

These were adrenaline thrills for him, and he quickly became bored with the tedious training flights he and his fellow pilots were required to do. Along with two friends, Locklear would regularly take a plane far out from the base and practice doing wild and dangerous stunts in the air.

He started by trying to walk on the lower wing of the biplane, moving from one strut to the other. Then he tried pulling himself up from the lower wing to the upper wing. On November 8, 1918, he tried—and succeeded—in transferring from one plane to another. As he hung from the lower wing of one, he was able to drop to the upper wing of the other craft as it flew slightly below. It is very likely that this was the first time anyone had succeeded in accomplishing this amazing feat.

Shortly after the war ended, Locklear left the air service and decided he could make a career out of stunt flying. He joined a bunch of "barnstormers" who were managed by William H. Pickens, a master event promoter. Originally the term "barnstormer" had applied to traveling actors who moved from town to town, often setting up temporary theaters in farmers' barns. The term was adopted by stunt flyers who would move about the country doing air exhibitions at county fairs.

With his wild and dangerous air acrobatics, Ormer Locklear soon became a sensation. Along with two former air service buddies, "Skeets" Elliott and Shirley Short, the three flyers toured the country at fairs and other outdoor events, flying above the crowd, with "Lock" doing his death-defying stunts, as the people below watched, gasping in terror.

In July 1919, Pickens made a deal with Carl Laemmle, president of the Universal Film Company, and, to the surprise of everyone—including Ormer—Pickens signed for him to head for Hollywood to star in a film to be called *The Great Air Robbery*. The film would incorporate many of the stunts Locklear had pioneered.

Once he got to Hollywood, Ormer Locklear, the charming young flyer, quickly became very popular with the film colony. Even though he had a wife named Ruby back in Texas, he became extremely friendly with actress Viola Dana, and frequently took her up for flights in his plane. They would fly low over Hollywood Boulevard, dropping small souvenirs to the crowds below. When Viola was working on a film, Ormer would think nothing of flying over to the studio, bouncing his plane off the roof of a building, and landing on nearby Cahuenga Boulevard.

When filming began on his film, *The Great Air Robbery,* Locklear's stunts were put to good use. Early in the movie, he does a transfer from one plane to another. In one of the final scenes (with a friend in the pilot's seat), they pursue a car with their plane flying directly above it. Then Ormer drops from the plane to the car, fights with the fleeing villain, and retrieves some stolen jewels. Now with the plane again hovering over the speeding car, Lock reaches up and pulls himself back up to the aircraft, just as the car crashes out of control and the villain meets his deserved end.

Once filming was completed, Ormer went back on the barnstorming circuit with the group he called "Locklear's Flying Circus," and in just four months in 1919 performed at 22 fairs and air shows in fifteen states. In keeping with his status as the top stunt flyer of his day, he would often command as much as $3000 for a day's work—an incredible amount of money for the time.

The Great Air Robbery opened in Los Angeles in December 1919, and the premiere was followed by a two-month tour with Ormer doing demonstration flights in each city where it opened.

With the success of the picture, Locklear felt he had a career with Laemmle's film company, but it was not to happen. Despite their original promises, no further movies were planned for him.

Hoping that a career in making films would help him avoid the pressure of another season of barnstorming, Ormer continued to spend his time in Hollywood trying to convince other producers to use his aerial talents. Finally in April 1920, he signed with the William Fox Studio to do a film to be called *The Skywayman*.

His salary would be $1650 per week, and he admitted he needed the money. The film was written by Jules Furthman, who would go on to a long and distinguished career in Hollywood, writing screenplays for *Morocco* (1930), *Blonde Venus* (1932), *To Have and Have Not* (1944), and *The Big Sleep* (1946)—among many others.

There would be a number of daring stunts to challenge Locklear, including climbing down a rope ladder from a plane onto a speeding train, crashing his aircraft through the steeple of a church, and hanging from a plane's landing gear while trading shots with some villains.

The final scene was to be a spectacular dive that would take place at night. In spite of the fact that Sol Wurtzel, superintendent of Fox Studios, wanted to film it "day for night," Ormer disagreed. Panchromatic film stock had recently been developed, and, the cameraman explained, by putting a red filter in front of the lens, scenes filmed in daylight looked just like night. But Locklear was a stickler for authenticity, and, perhaps, a compulsive daredevil. He insisted that he do the scene after dark, and he and "Skeets" Elliott even did a test flight one night, performing some stunts to prove he could work just as well in the darkness.

The date was Monday, August 2nd. It was the night they would do the final scene for *The Skywayman*. Locklear and Viola Dana had a leisurely dinner at the Hollywood Hotel then drove to the airfield. Three cameras had been set up and several powerful arc lamps were in place to film the dive. A crowd had assembled to see the exciting sequence.

The men operating the arc lamps had been instructed to shut them off when Locklear had descended to 500 feet as a signal it was time to pull out of the dive.

At 9:40 p.m. "Skeets" and Ormer took off into the night sky. In ten minutes they had reached 3000 feet and the huge arcs were turned on filling the sky with beams of light. After fifteen minutes of rolls and loops in the brilliant light of the arcs, it was time for the dive. At 10:05 Ormer flipped the switch for the magnesium flares and the crowd below gasped at the brilliant illumination coming off the plane. Down came the spinning aircraft.

But for some strange reason, the bright arc lights were never extinguished.

And the plane never pulled out of its dive.

The Jenny crashed into a mound of earth surrounding an oil sump and its occupants were flung out. In a moment there was an explosion, and the magnesium flares ignited the oil into a flaming inferno.

When the bodies of Elliot and Locklear were finally able to be retrieved, someone noticed the smashed wristwatch on Ormer's wrist. The broken timepiece had stopped at 10:14.

The funeral cortege for Elliott and Locklear was unmatched in Hollywood history: There was a twenty-four-piece band, an honor guard, twenty mounted cowboys, and twelve pallbearers who marched beside the hearses. Eighteen planes flew overhead, dropping thousands of rose petals, and the Goodyear blimp floated above it all.

While a bugler blew taps, the caskets were loaded onto a train to return the fallen flyers to their respective hometowns.

Little more than a month later Fox rushed *The Sky-wayman* into theaters, and it even included the final dive in which Skeets and Lock had perished. Though hardly averse to exploitation, the film company did announce it would give ten percent of all profits from the film to the families of the two flyers.

While the days of barnstorming would continue for some years after Omer Locklear's death and would cost the lives of several more pilots, stunt flying and wing walking ultimately became a thing of the past. It was, however, briefly remembered in the film, *The Great Waldo Pepper,* made in 1975, starring Robert Redford. It was a film that vividly recalled those exciting days of rickety aircraft and the daring pilots who flew them.

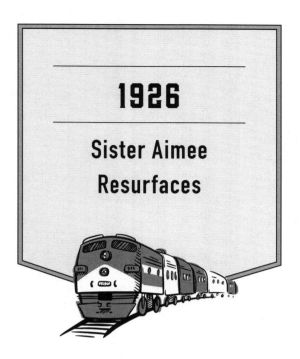

1926

Sister Aimee
Resurfaces

What a triumphant return it was—Sister Aimee, back from the dead! At the railway station happy crowds laid down a carpet of roses. They had waited for hours to get just one glimpse of the plump, smiling mother of two. One hundred thousand people cheered her, their spiritual leader, as she stepped off the train and made her way along a parade route through Los Angeles. The red-haired woman was nearly as pink and pretty as the flowers she carried in her arms. She clasped her hands and looked heavenward as twenty duded-up cowboys and a brass band escorted her home.

Even skeptics had to admit that Aimee Semple McPherson knew how to make an entrance—and an exit. Just eight days before her triumphant return, the beloved founder of the Four Square Gospel Church had walked into the ocean and not come up for air. She had drowned. At least that's what her friends and followers on the beach thought. One minute Aimee was going in swimming, and the next she was nowhere to be seen.

The Four Square members had panicked at the thought of the queen of their faith gasping for air. Boats and swimmers searched the strand but found no sign of their beloved leader. One of the faithful even drowned in the process. All of Los Angeles believed Sister Aimee was dead.

So it was a miracle when their lost leader reappeared at the Mexican border. The vibrant evangelist had a horrific story to tell. She claimed she had been kidnapped, and only with great effort had she managed to escape. After such perilous adventures, she deserved a triumphant homecoming.

The first time Sister Aimee arrived in Los Angeles, it was with considerably less fuss. A young widow with two children to feed, she came west as a preacher. She had ten dollars in her pocket and lived in tent camps. Los Angeles was swollen with Midwesterners who wanted some kind of spiritual guidance, and Sister Aimee gave it to them. She also threw in a little bit of spectacle as she preached, to hold the crowds: stabbing a man in a devil suit with a pitchfork, for instance, or hiring budding musicians to give a little bit of sway to the service. In a short time, Aimee gathered a loyal congregation. She also took in plenty of money, enough to make her church swell. Angelus Temple was the Four Square church's visible manifestation of the heavenly kingdom—a $1.5 million shrine with five thousand seats, built entirely from donations.

Sister Aimee worked hard, but that alone didn't explain her appeal. From the studios of radio station KFSG, her voice sounded ragged, but it could also bend a warble with every emotion. She spoke over the airwaves two or three times each day, and her listeners numbered in the thousands. She never claimed to be able to heal the sick, but she would pray for anyone who asked her.

Aimee looked like a saint as she marched back into the town that had built her up. But newspaper reporters who had traced her tracks in Mexico told another story. They said that Aimee had run off to meet a lover and had hoped for a Mexican marriage. When she could not give them details about the alleged kidnapping, police arrested the curvaceous church leader and charged her with giving false information. The media smelled scandal, and went for blood. They ran lurid stories and printed rumors until Sister Aimee went to trial—where the charges were dropped.

Some said the whole affair was a giant publicity stunt. If so, it worked. Sister Aimee's followers loved her even more after her return from the dead. They especially loved her when she wore the white admiral's suit that reminded them she'd nearly been lost at sea. She even managed to upstage the military at a celebration of Los Angeles' 150th birthday, gaining more applause than the troops. By 1944, when she died, the reverend mother of the Four Square Gospel Church had started more than two hundred chapels and given all of Southern California a show to remember.

1929

A Stately
Pleasure Dome

The young man on the clarinet adjusted his wire-rimmed glasses, set his foot tapping, and rent the air with a lament of love. As the music hovered over cigarette girls dressed in red and yellow satin, it wrapped itself around the dancing couples. The music and mood lighting turned the Casino Ballroom into a pink and mahogany cloud. To the sounds of Benny Goodman and his twenty-piece band, young lovers danced until their arms ached—but their feet waltzed and did the fox-trot all night long. On the springy ballroom floor, the happy dancers were floating on air. "I met my love in Avalon," they could sing, "across the sea!"

The ballroom actually did hang in midair, suspended in space. The dance hall was the centerpiece of a ten-story palace built for play. Its floating floor was architectural magic.

Layer upon layer of wood, cork, and foam were suspended from the sides of the immense cream-colored Casino Building on Catalina Island. The ballroom's large circular floor had no pillars or beams underneath, nothing that propped it up from below. William Wrigley Jr. and his architects had used the principle of the cantilever, allowing the weight of the floor to be borne by the walls. Without a rigid base, the polished wood floor could give slightly. With a light step and the right swing band, a couple could dance there for hours without tiring.

William Wrigley Jr. had spared no expense in creating his fantasy ballroom. Founder of the company that made minty Wrigley's Chewing Gum, he appreciated the need for fun and could afford to indulge his dreams. He had a vacation home on Santa Catalina Island, a romantic hideaway only twenty-two miles from mainland California. A former resting place for smugglers along the Southern California coast, the island had drawn tourists since the mid-nineteenth century. Wrigley already turned a profit by running glass-bottomed boats that crisscrossed the clear waters of the island's main harbor. He saw that vacationers supported the Avalon Tuna Club, where famous sport fishermen talked about prize catches and conserving yellowfins. From Catalina's crescent-shaped cove, he looked up at the town called Avalon and knew that it was ripe for an even more glamorous kind of amusement. Sports fan, banker, and man of industry, Wrigley decided to give the "lotus-eaters" of Southern California a new pleasure dome.

The suspended floor of the Casino Ballroom was only one of the building's novelties. Socialites ascended the nine floors to the ballroom not on stairs but on plush-carpeted stadium ramps. The gentle climb was easy for ladies in long dresses and left even heavy men with enough energy to dance. Wrigley took the idea from Wrigley Field, his sports arena in Chicago, home of the Chicago Cubs baseball team. If the Casino's sophisticated visitors had looked closely at the cream-colored building, they might have seen that it resembled an Art Deco stadium with a few fancy added details.

For those who didn't want to dance, the Casino Building had a Moorish-style balcony with views of Avalon Harbor and massive Sugarloaf Rock, perfect for moonlight strolls. Its mezzanine offered soda fountains and lounging areas. Wrigley's pleasure dome also housed a gigantic theater where visitors could listen to the giant pipe organ or view one of the many new "talkie" motion pictures beneath a ceiling lit by artificial stars. Under that imaginary night sky, or in the carpeted mezzanine corridors lit by translucent shell lamps, glamorous women and princely men could enter a fantasy world.

The Casino Ballroom was removed from reality in more ways than one. Wrigley's new building opened in autumn 1929, just moments before the nation hit economic hard times. Some of Wrigley's guests were wealthy enough to avoid the crush of the Great Depression, but for many who visited the beautiful dance floor with its bouncy, suspended floor, these nights were the last of the age of play.

Wrigley's monument to fun still stands at the side of Avalon Harbor, with a restored interior and a museum in its basement. It is a favorite location for films and advertising videos, and each year it draws thousands of tourists who dream of dancing on air.

1933

Long Beach Shakes

On a still, muggy evening in Long Beach during the Great Depression, when every disaster seemed like yet another sign that the world would soon end, the earth moved. Palm trees leapt into the air. Hens supposedly laid large numbers of eggs. The sky, a mass of black clouds, seemed to boil. Buildings swayed out of sight, reappeared, then swayed in the other direction. Men and small boys were lifted twenty feet into the air. Some said the most amazing sight that night was the local bootleggers spreading good cheer in the aftermath, passing out illegal whiskey for free.

LaRee Caughey had just turned from the stove with her family's supper when the earth rolled up and took it away. The ocean floor near Long Beach had shifted along a fault in the earth's crust, causing the entire region to dip slightly toward the sea. The earthquake's shock waves hit so fast that some people could not register what was happening. They saw explosions or black space in their brains. The Caugheys' soup pot rode out the roller coaster without ever tipping over: the ground that had surged up to pick it from the cook's hands placed it upright, just as quickly, on the kitchen linoleum.

When the shaking stopped, the entire Los Angeles Basin froze amid the howls of dogs and the cries of children. Southern California realized that it had just been shaken like never before. Buildings in Compton and Long Beach—especially schools—lay in ruins. By the next morning, officials counted more than a hundred dead and estimated $50 million in property damage.

At 6.3 on the Richter scale, the March 10, 1933 earthquake was one hundred times less severe than San Francisco's disastrous 1906 quake. But Long Beach had not thought it could happen to them. Town promoters had sworn that the big quakes would hit the northern parts of the state rather than the cities along the sunshine coast. Construction had catered to the no-quake dream: brick was the favorite material for storefronts, and taller buildings had overhanging stone rims. All these blocks of burned clay and carved rock had tumbled to the streets with the land's first twitch.

Angelenos were shocked to learn from Dr. Harry Wood, a Cal Tech professor who testified to the coroner's jury, that even worse shaking could happen at any time. Part of the trouble lay in the fact that Long Beach was a city built on sand and clay. Its oceanfront property sat on oil pools and groundwater, with nothing solid to anchor it or absorb a blow. The ground there could ripple at will. The harbor town had been lucky this time: the quake's epicenter was several miles offshore.

Since that March day in 1933, people throughout the Southland have thought of humid, quiet days as "earthquake weather." A more important and scientific result of the Long Beach quake was a change in building codes. No longer would Southern California classrooms be built without ceiling and window reinforcements; government buildings of the future would not rely on cheap brick and unsupported plaster. Within two years, the California legislature had passed the Field Act, the toughest building code in the nation, hoping to keep the state's public structures safe—until the next, larger quake arrives.

1934

The Lettuce Harvest

At the first explosion, oily vapors seeped into the dilapidated meeting room. Outside, policemen waited by the doors to arrest any of the lettuce pickers who tried to flee the tear gas fumes. "As of this morning, union meetings are illegal in the Imperial Valley," the law officers shouted. "You're under arrest."

"What are you talking about?" yelled back one of the union representatives, nearly choking on the smoke. "We have the right to peaceably assemble."

"Not if you're striking, you don't," a deputy said. "This morning the county government made all union meetings against the law."

Amid clouds of gas punctuated by a few bullets, confusion reigned. The lettuce pickers of the Imperial Valley began to sense how powerless they really were, no matter what the U.S. Constitution said. They were used to hardship, but they had not known the extremes to which the lettuce growers would go in order to protect their business.

California was the nation's top agricultural state, which meant that it was also the top employer of seasonal harvesters. The Imperial Valley's lettuce and vegetable pickers were mostly immigrant Mexicans, who worked for low wages and lived in temporary work camps. The pickers had always expected to work hard. They had known that life in the camps would be difficult. But poverty had knocked too many times at their doors. To them, it appeared that the farmers reaped the profits of their forced labor.

Workers' wages depended on how much lettuce they could gather; theoretically, they might make four hundred dollars a year, if they worked full time. But the pickers could not count on full-time labor. The work was seasonal, and the crews often spent only twenty hours a week in the fields. Then, after a crop was in, some contractors refused to pay them in full, or delayed their wages until the crop was sold.

Most of the workers lived in small villages called *colonias,* or "little Mexicos." Some growers had built small eighteen-by-twenty-two-foot cottages to house the people who performed the essential task of harvest. The laborers traveled from farm to farm with their families and rented the thin-walled houses for $7.50 a month. In the best places the shacks had inner walls, running water, heat, and toilets. In the worst, they were just wooden shells near an outhouse. As the Great Depression wore on, the pickers saw more of the worst kind.

Within these camps, the workers did their best to create a sense of community. The women sewed their own clothing and started small businesses on the side. The camps had baseball teams and celebrated Mexican holidays, especially Diez y Seis, Mexican Independence Day, on the sixteenth of September. The *colonias* were isolated from the world at large, but they became close-knit islands of Spanish language and Latino culture.

In spite of the successes of some, many Mexican pickers struggled to survive. The lettuce pickers had banded together so that they could ask for better wages. When the Cannery and Agricultural Workers Industrial Union (CAWIU) of California called for a general strike of lettuce and vegetable pickers in January 1934, many men from the Imperial Valley joined the picket lines.

The Imperial Valley growers reacted badly. They saw efforts to improve their workers' lives as a threat to their own livelihoods—after all, they needed cheap labor for cheap crops, and their profits depended on a timely harvest. Perhaps with some reluctance, they responded with violence to the idea of unionization. They also capitalized on language barriers, wanting English only for any legal arrangements. They passed local laws against assembly or picketing, then called in the police as thugs. Area newspapers went along with such tactics, spreading rumors that the lettuce pickers had been brainwashed by Communists. All this served the growers' real purpose: getting low-paid workers back in the fields.

That night in January 1934, policemen rounded up eighty strikers with tear gas. Immediately, without taking necessary legal steps, they marched the workers toward the Mexican border. Any who tried to run would be shot by armed guards, the authorities threatened. Their eyes and noses still stinging from the gas clouds, the men were forced to walk without relief until, midway to the border, they were told to stop. There, in front of them, stood the Mexican consul, Joaquin Terrazas. With eloquence he urged them to cancel the strike before they were forced across the international line.

Terrazas was to be believed, since he himself oversaw immigration at the border station in Caléxico. Sly and ingratiating, he was also the growers' best weapon. Never mind that as a Mexican national he knew nothing about U.S. labor law—or that he was known to be corrupt. In an earlier conflict in the Imperial Valley, Terrazas had talked farm workers into going back to work by promising to tell growers how hard their lives were. Instead, when he did talk to the growers, he blamed union organizers and suggested the striking workers had been misled.

But Terrazas's threats were not as idle as his promises. "Whether you are here legally or illegally, I can send you back and no one will know the difference," he said. Speaking with pretended conviction he added, "I'm on your side. I've got your best interests at heart. Trust me."

What choice did the workers have? Terrazas was not their friend, but they would do their families no good by being deported. The lettuce pickers of southeastern California had not imagined they would be gassed or threatened with deportation for speaking up about their wages. The lettuce harvest went on as planned. Violence and blackmail had paid off for the growers.

Two months later, after the harvests were in, the parties agreed to talk. In March 1934, with the support of the CAWIU, they sat down at last to discuss wages. The Mexican workers agreed to tend the fields for twenty-five cents an hour—ten cents less than they had asked for at the start. But they bought this small gain at an outrageous price. They had to agree never to strike, no matter what conditions the growers imposed. If they even thought of forming a new union, the violence would begin all over again.

California had a reputation as America's top producer of farm crops, but few knew what credit was due to the Mexican immigrants and their ability to succeed in spite of everything. It took years of struggle before the valley's labor environment changed and immigrant workers were able to reclaim their consitutional rights.

1940

Message Movie
Makes Money

"If you want to send a message, don't make a movie, use Western Union."

Whoever was the Hollywood mogul who said this was echoing the sentiments of a host of film producers and studio owners over the years. For them movies were for entertainment, entertainment brought in audiences, and that meant money at the box office. For them "message pictures" were usually the kiss of death.

Yet, every now and then, there were exceptions. Not the least of these was a film made from a novel by author John Steinbeck. In 1937 Steinbeck went to Detroit, bought a car, and drove to Oklahoma. Next he joined a group of migrant farmers who were heading to California, driven out of their homes by drought, dust storms, and their inability to keep up rent payments because of poor crops. He lived with them and worked with them in the fields and then he decided to tell their story in a novel he would call *The Grapes of Wrath.*

The book, which followed one family (he called the Joads) and depicted their problems and treatment in their trek west, was published in March 1939 and was an instant success, staying on the best-seller list month after month. But because it was a story that pulled no punches, many places banned it, calling the novel subversive and obscene.

In 1939 Darryl F. Zanuck was in charge of production at Twentieth-Century Fox Studios. Thirty-seven years old at the time, Zanuck had had a rapid rise to success in the film business. He had joined the army in 1917 (he lied about the fact that he was only fourteen) and served in France. After the war, he had a host of part-time jobs, but he was interested in being a writer. He sold some stories to the movies in 1922, worked for a time with comedy director Mack Sennett, and eventually was hired at Warner Brothers Studios to write for one of their biggest stars: the dog called Rin Tin Tin. He wrote prolifically, often using pseudonyms, and in the brief five-year period from 1924 to 1929 turned out more than forty scripts. By 1931 he had moved up the ladder and was promoted to head of production. In 1933 he joined with Joseph Schenck and William Goetz to found a new company, eventually called Twentieth Century Fox.

Zanuck was not averse to making "message pictures," as long as they proved to be profitable. He would make *How Green Was My Valley* in 1941, about the tribulations of Welsh coal miners, and would be responsible for the films *Gentleman's Agreement* (1947) about antisemitism and *Pinky* (1949) that dealt with racial intolerance.

Zanuck had his studio buy the film rights to Steinbeck's book for $70,000. But before he decided to make the film, he hired a private investigating firm to see if there was any truth to some of the things the novelist had presented: migrants abused and beaten, workers forced to live in unbearable housing, people made to work long hours in the fields at wages of pennies an hour.

The investigators brought back their report: the truth was even worse than what Steinbeck had presented in his book.

Zanuck chose staff writer Nunnally Johnson to write the screenplay. He had worked at the studio for several years and had written some successful films. Johnson had a major challenge ahead of him since the book not only follows the Joad family but also has chapters that are documentary in content, giving a general picture of what was happening to other families and highlighting many of the indignities heaped on the migrants by those who took advantage of their plight. The writer also had to do away with all the profanity in the book (it was 1939 and the Hays Office made the studios adhere strictly to the Production Code).

Johnson's other problem was the ending. In the book the Joads' daughter is pregnant and when she finally delivers the baby, it is stillborn. Yet she saves the life of a starving man by giving her mother's milk to him from her breast. This scene, symbolic of how the migrants helped each other for survival, was definitely not a scene that could be shown in a film.

Instead Johnson pulled a scene from earlier in the book where the family is well treated at a government camp, and, as they leave to look for work, Ma Joad says, "We'll go on forever, Pa. We're the people." The movie ends with at least this suggestion of hope.

Since the book had been so controversial, filming it was done in strictest secrecy. Zanuck had supposedly gotten thousands of letters, most of which said he would never make the film since the studios were allied with big business, and big business as represented by the banks and large farm owners were the ones most criticized in the story. In addition, some states like Oklahoma and Arkansas would have resisted letting the filmmakers use their locations because they were portrayed as poverty-stricken environments where living conditions for many sharecroppers were close to intolerable.

A film crew was sent out to film locations and background, but they were told to say that the production they were shooting was a totally different film called *Highway 66,* and most of the actual shooting was done on sound stages at Twentieth Century Fox.

A valuable addition to the production was photographer Gregg Toland (who would also film *Citizen Kane*), but for *The Grapes of Wrath* his images were much more gritty and realistic, copying a style similar to documentary films made in the thirties.

The cast, which included Henry Fonda as Tom Joad, Jane Darwell as Ma (she would win an Academy Award as best actress), and John Carradine as the "preacher" Joe Casy, provided the right tone for the film. The direction by John Ford was also just right for the material. Ford's skill in translating the script to the screen may have something to do with his comment years later (whether truthful or not) that, "I never read the book." Ford also claimed to be totally apolitical and his interest in doing the film stemmed from his Irish heritage and the story's similarity to that of the poor Irish farmers who had been thrown off their land.

It is also interesting to note that those involved in making *The Grapes of Wrath* were not politically liberal or progressive: Nunnally Johnson claimed to be conservative and Zanuck said he generally voted Republican. Yet it was a story that appealed to them all, by virtue of its characters and its strong theme of survival in spite of tremendous adversity.

When author John Steinbeck saw the film, he was quite impressed. He was quoted in a letter to his agent as saying that the film is even harsher than his book and "has a hard, truthful ring." He even said that it felt like a documentary film.

Made at a cost of $850,000, *The Grapes of Wrath* received generally outstanding reviews and did excellent business. It was the studio's biggest success of the year.

The enduring success of *The Grapes of Wrath* was, perhaps, best summed up by author Rudy Behlmer in his book, *America's Favorite Movies: Behind the Scenes* when he wrote: ". . . the theme, the structure, the ideas, the emotions, and specifically the sentiments . . . are timeless and relate to no particular geography. The family sticking together despite overwhelming problems, the migration to the Promised Land, obstacles along the way, gradual disenchantment, the exploitation of simple and good people, the tenacity—the 'We're the people' philosophy, and above all the love of land and family—these elements all endure."

1942

Documenting Manzanar

Kango Takamura had a job at RKO Studios in Hollywood. His work was not glamorous—printing and retouching pictures—but he hoped to be a cameraman someday. When his boss asked him to meet with a man from Japan to talk about selling several of the studio's movie cameras, he was glad for the extra responsibility. He did not expect to be arrested as a spy.

In December 1941, the Imperial Japanese Army bombed the American naval base at Pearl Harbor, Hawaii, bringing the United States into World War II. Late one night, two months later, federal investigators knocked on the door of Takamura's family home in Los Angeles and arrested him. He was immediately sent to an "enemy alien" prison camp on suspicion of trying to sell cameras to the Japanese military.

Born in Japan, Takamura had immigrated to Hawaii then New York before settling in Southern California. He had dreamed of being a painter when he was young, but he later changed his mind and chose the camera as his medium. He liked the idea of an art form that documented the world as it changed.

The job at RKO was a good one, but after Pearl Harbor it led the cameraman into trouble. In 1942, Takamura and thousands of other Japanese Americans fell under suspicion, especially those who had access to technology that might be used by enemy spies—cameras, for instance. On that night of arrests, the Federal Bureau of Investigation (FBI) took the young RKO photographer and his cameras away. A thousand other suspected spies were jailed, too. (Later, separate investigations were conducted, one by the FBI and one by the Federal Communications Commission. Neither organization found a single example of espionage or sabotage on the part of Japanese Americans.)

Though he had done nothing wrong, Takamura was sent inland to Santa Fe, New Mexico. There he waited for the U.S. government to finish building internment camps that would hold all the American Japanese until the war was over. Kango couldn't believe that the government would jail more than 120,000 people. It seemed like something that could happen only in the movies.

In the summer of 1942, Takamura was moved back to California, where he joined his family at a place called Manzanar. The camp was a collection of barracks enclosed by wire fences in the shadow of the eastern Sierra. Two stone guardhouses waited at its gate, and beyond them rose the long dormitories, covered with black tarpaper. Thin ventilation pipes poked up from the roofs. On the windswept flat, no vegetation grew at all. In place of trees were only electric wires and poles.

Japanese Americans in California were stunned by their sudden relocation. The same month that Takamura was arrested, notices posted on telephone poles and store windows told them to pack only what they could carry for the move to relocation centers. The U.S. government had frozen the bank accounts of *Issei,* Japanese Americans who had been born in Japan; most had to sell their furniture or cars for cash. *Nisei,* American-born citizens of Japanese descent, were the most confused—they had been brought up as Americans, listening to big band music and playing team sports. They spoke English and went to public school. They couldn't imagine any reason for the government to suspect them. Yet they, too, were forced to live surrounded by wire and guarded by troops. There were no easy answers for these American citizens.

Takamura moved among the people at Manzanar and saw their bewildered faces. He had not forgotten his dream of documenting world events. He had no camera, but he still had pencil and paper. Drawing cartoons, he soon learned to sketch all parts of camp life. He wanted to leave a record of the people who had survived in an era of unjustified suspicion.

The camp offered little privacy, and the cramped quarters had only cots and simple furniture, whatever its residents could make from crates. But many who lived there endured bravely and gained character. At Manzanar, the residents built a stone garden with benches near a pond. They made small, decorative pieces of plastic jewelry from melted toothbrush handles and carved faces in cypress wood as a means of beautifying their stark surroundings.

Takamura's art was more practical. He drew pictures of the camp residents who earned twelve dollars a month doing manual labor for the U.S. government. He sketched the women who cleared sagebrush, or the men who harvested guayule, a rubber substitute, in nearby fields. All ten thousand people in camp were his subjects, from young boys in t-shirts to old women in the traditional sandals called *getas*.

The young photographer hid his sketches at first. He was afraid the military guards or the War Relocation Authority would think that he was up to something. But no one seemed to mind, so Takamura brought his pictures out and added watercolor to them. Art was his way of refusing to give up freedom.

At the end of World War II, after three years in prison camps like Manzanar, Japanese Americans were allowed to go back to their former homes. Still, life was never the same for them again. Many of their homes had been sold, and their assets lost. They were still viewed with suspicion by the larger population, mostly because they looked like the enemy the nation had just defeated.

Takamura's sketches are still among the best records of life at the camps. Although famous photographers such as Dorothea Lange and Ansel Adams came to visit Manzanar, the sketches of a Japanese-born cameraman who lived there tell more about the camp than the best of their images.

1942

Capra Explains "Why We Fight"

December 7, 1941: Pearl Harbor had been bombed and America was in the war.

Suddenly, for everyone, life had changed. Education, career, marital plans, all were put on hold. No one knew how long it would last, how many sacrifices would have to be made, what dangers lay ahead. But one thing was clear: the war had come to us, and it had to be fought.

Millions of young men—and women—would soon be part of a vast effort to prepare a massive force of soldiers, sailors, and airmen, to equip them, train them, and send them off to places around the world. A great deal had to be done and the time was short.

Frank Capra was forty-five years old, much older than most of those enlisting in the military, but he chose to serve, and was quickly commissioned as a major in the Signal Corps, the unit that produced training films. Yet he did not look forward to spending his time grinding out footage on how to service a rifle or how to put on a gas mask. He had already directed some outstanding (and Academy Award–winning) productions, and he was known as a mover and shaker, as well as a tough man to deal with. He had confronted the sometimes intractable forces in Hollywood, and now he was ready to contend with a still larger, more immovable entity called the U.S. Army, and it would indeed prove to be a major challenge.

In short order Capra was summoned to the office of General George C. Marshall, the Army's Chief of Staff, and a man whose career both in the military, and after the war, as Secretary of State, would have a major effect on the world.

General Marshall's instructions to Capra were succinct and to the point. He wanted a series of factual-information films that would be shown to the men and women in uniform, films that explained why we were fighting and the principles for which we were fighting. He explained that the films would be a top priority.

Frank Capra had never made a documentary film before, but he took the order from General Marshall to heart. He decided that he would use every facility he could beg, borrow, or steal and every resource he could muster to put together a series of productions that could well have an important role in the war effort.

But first he looked at what the enemy had produced. He had a copy of the Nazi propaganda film *Triumph of the Will* shown to him. Made by skilled film maker Leni Riefenstahl several years before, it was a bone-chilling look at the deification of Adolf Hitler as he spoke to the assembled believers at the Nuremberg Congress in 1934. It was a film that no doubt had won over many to Hitler's cause by its repetitious scenes of shouting masses and blind allegiance to the almost god-like presence of Hitler, the Fuhrer.

With propaganda like this film to combat, Capra knew he had his work cut out for him. He finally hit on an idea that would serve him well as the basis for the series of motion pictures that would become *Why We Fight.* He would use excerpts from the enemy's own propaganda films to show what they were doing and what their intentions were. This would clearly demonstrate their desire for world domination and how they intended to accomplish it.

He went on a search and after being referred from one office to another, finally came upon a treasure trove of years of confiscated enemy footage. Even more important, he realized that he had to divest himself of control by the Signal Corps whose general insisted that all decisions and production had to be under his authority. After some heated confrontations, Capra was able to get a memo stating that he would run a special detachment under the control not of the Signal Corps, but of the Chief of Special Services. Thus the 834th Photo Signal Detachment was born, and Capra would be able to begin work without interference.

He envisaged seven films, each fifty-minutes in length: the first was *Prelude to War,* illustrating (with graphics and film clips) the rise of Japanese and Italian militarism; the second, *The Nazis Strike,* which shows Hitler's rise to power, his takeover of Germany, Austria, Czechoslovakia, and Poland; the third, *Divide and Conquer,* which shows Hitler's war machine as it overcomes Denmark, Norway, and France; the fourth film is called *Battle of Britain,* depicting the gallant British as they fight off the Nazi attack; the fifth, *Battle of Russia,* describes how the German army is finally beaten back at Stalingrad; the sixth, *Battle of China,* presents Japan's overthrow of the Chinese mainland and its intention to dominate all of Asia.

The last of the series was *War Comes to America.* This film was a brief visual history of the United States and its democratic values; how our feelings of non-involvement in others' affairs gradually changed to a realization that loss of freedoms anywhere was a threat to the freedoms we enjoyed.

Was Capra making propaganda, American style? Absolutely. But it was strong and convincing and told a story that was critically needed at this most important moment in history. What else Capra was doing was simplifying a highly complex series of historical events. These were films designed to be shown to servicemen, most of whom had very limited education. And though, many years later, he was criticized for his approach, these movies were exactly what was needed at this critical point in our history.

The approach was simple and to the point. In *Prelude to War,* the narrator says, "This is a common man's life-and-death struggle against those who would put him back into slavery. We lose it—and we lose everything. Our homes, the jobs we want to go back to, the books we read, the very food we eat, the hopes we have for our kids, the kids themselves— they won't be ours anymore. That's what's at stake. It's us or them. The chips are down."

Capra utilized not only enemy news film but often footage lifted from feature films as well. He justified this by saying that, in many cases, this was all that was available. But many of the wartime feature films depicted the Japanese and Germans as stereotypical (almost buffoonish) villains.

Yet he clearly understood what he was doing, and, even though he was propagandizing, he was doing it for a just cause, and the defeat of the enemy was his primary reason for making the films.

Using all the resources he could muster, Capra was able to move into the Western Avenue Twentieth Century Studios in Hollywood, and borrow and acquire equipment for his production unit. Being this far from Washington kept the brass away from him and helped to ensure his independence.

When the first of the series, *Prelude to War,* was completed, Capra was summoned to be present when President Franklin Roosevelt screened it. With considerable trepidation, he met the president and sat down in the room with him as the film was projected. The last caption, superimposed over the faces of marching soldiers, reads, "No compromise is possible and the victory of the democracies can only be complete with the utter defeat of the war machines of Germany and Japan.—G.C. Marshall, Chief of Staff."

As the lights came up, there was applause, and the president said, "Every man, woman, and child in the world must see this film."

Eventually, some of the films in the *Why We Fight* series were shown to general audiences, although they were mainly intended for the military. They were also shown in other countries to the public and translated into a number of languages.

At the March 1943 Academy Awards ceremony, four films were given awards as best documentaries of the year. Capra's *Prelude to War* was one of those honored.

Frank Capra and his film unit would go on to make a number of documentary films for the army. Whether or not his pictures had a major effect on the troops and their morale and understanding has often been open to question. But it has always been acknowledged that what Capra did, he did well.

When he left the military after the war ended and returned to Hollywood, he discovered, unhappily, that film-making had changed in many ways, and it was the stars, not the directors who were in charge.

He did, however, make one film after the war that, while not successful initially, has become a true classic of American cinema: the Christmas classic *It's a Wonderful Life*.

1943

A Riveting Experiment

Eager to clock in at work on Monday morning, Doris pushed down the lock on her green Ford sedan's door and eased it shut. As soon as the heavy metal clicked, however, she realized she had left her safety glasses on the front seat. As she opened the Ford's door with a creak, her young son woke up.

"Are you on a break, Mommy?" he asked.

"No, honey, I'm just going in now. Be a good boy today, okay?"

The boy murmured a kind of yes as he fell back asleep in the predawn light. The young mother smoothed her son's disheveled hair and straightened his blanket on the back seat before she closed the door again and walked into the camouflaged aircraft plant in time for her shift.

Consolidated Vultee's accordion-pleated roof was draped with netting, and Doris was dressed for war work, too. She wore a demin shirt, dungarees, and a kerchief on her head. Her shift as a riveter would take her through the next ten hours. She did not mind the challenge of working for wages, but like the other mothers she did not relish the idea of leaving her son alone all day in the car. They all did it; they had to. The war effort required that everyone pitch in, and the Germans would not wait for plant workers to organize childcare.

The job with Vultee was the first Doris had held since her marriage. It was nearly five years ago that she had earned a paycheck as a soda fountain girl in high school. In her current job, the young soldier's wife had learned how to operate a rivet gun and connect cut pieces of aluminum on an airplane's streamlined hull. She had even been promoted within the company and had helped to train new employees. On good days, she hoped that her job might continue after the war was over—with better facilities for children, of course. Her son was only two years old, but in another year he would be too old to leave in the car alone. He might figure out how to open the door by himself.

Doris had grown up right here in San Diego, but thousands of other workers had come to Southern California from all parts of the country. The war meant thousands of men and women had to pitch in. In California alone, 300,000 people were needed to make planes. Since most of the nation's able young men had been drafted or joined up to fight, older men and women of all ages—girls, mothers, sisters—had started new jobs on the assembly lines. Twenty-five thousand women had begun training at plants in San Diego County, and many of them had young children or infants.

San Diego's mild, sunny weather meant that the young women could leave their toddlers in their cars without worrying whether they'd get too cold or too hot. The climate also made San Diego a perfect place to build aircraft. The bay saw as many as 350 clear days a year, perfect conditions for test flying. When American soldiers went overseas, the federal government allocated $150 million to keep them flying high. The money went into new aircraft plants like Consolidated Vultee, and the soldiers' wives took their places on the assembly line.

Doris liked her new job and the income it brought, but she could not stop thinking about her young son and his safety. The Vultee parking lot was guarded, but her son had no one to watch him closely. Women with children took turns checking on all the kids at their breaks. They changed babies' diapers and read stories in ten-minute intervals and at lunch. In one parking lot, perhaps fifty babies and toddlers could be found in cars, waiting for their mothers' shifts to end.

Vultee's young workers learned to balance work and family as best they could. They were especially proud when aerospace pioneer Donald Douglas recognized their efforts, praising the industry's new, energetic employees. "We are an army of hundreds of thousands of aircraft workers with one aim only—victory," he had said. He added that people working side by side showed true democracy at work. "The layman looks at a Flying Fortress and sees one sleek, streamlined machine. An aircraft builder looks at the same Flying Fortress and sees 110,000 separate parts, welded and riveted together by thousands of men and women, most of whom never saw the inside of a bomber until less than a year ago."

Consolidated Vultee made sure its employees had plenty of time on the job to learn to do what was necessary. The company's president had asked the Secretary of the Navy and the California legislature to let women work overtime and on shifts that started late at night. But they still couldn't fill the orders for new planes. Doris hoped she and her son would be able to make do until the conflict ended.

Like other wartime workers, the young mother described here—a composite and not a specific individual—may have felt that she was part of something larger, a grand adventure or important mission. Although women like Doris would be relieved to see their husbands return from the war, they would speak of missing the excitement and sense of purpose that their jobs gave them. Postwar, they were encouraged to return home and become ideal homemakers, with all the benefits of new technology. During the conflict, they had been part of a wartime experiment that had a direct impact on women's work lives. In future years, no one could suggest that women in California weren't suited for industrial work. They'd held traditionally male jobs, and they'd helped their country gear up for war.

1947

The Chase

It was two in the morning when the man with the saxophone made his way down Central Avenue in Los Angeles to Jack Jackson's place, The Bird in the Basket. "Chicken ain't nuten but a bird" read a sign on the wall. The door opened for the musician as if he were royalty. "Dexter, come on it!" someone said. "We were just leaving, but we'll stay awhile if you're on. Dexter Gordon's here, everybody."

The mighty sax player easily lifted the sack that held his tenor instrument over the tables, where rattan baskets and greasy napkins marked a revolving feast. The smell of tobacco and cracklings hovered around the remains.

Gordon tipped his hat to the folks he knew as he made his way toward the low stage. He'd grown up in Los Angeles, and he recognized many of the night-owls' faces. "Are you ready to play like a demon?" one of his father's friends shouted out to him.

"Like an angel," the well-dressed Gordon answered. "Every night of my life. Bring 'em on."

Once on the platform, the saxophonist saw he wouldn't be playing alone. A group of sidemen—an alto sax player, a man with a bass, and a drummer—sat in the shadows, assembling instruments and adjusting rickety seats. But Gordon wasn't focusing on them. There, on the other side of the rattling box Jack called a piano, was a man opposite in most aspects to the city's native son. A tall, gangly skeleton, he was the man Gordon had come to meet.

Nicknamed the "Thin Man," Wardell Gray played the tenor sax, too, but there ended the similarities between him and Dexter Gordon. Slim and lightweight, Gray seemed to have grown his charcoal line of a mustache just to give him a little swinging weight. He was not the local favorite; instead of socializing, he spent his time with books, and he talked philosophy or race politics in a soft voice that was rare in the Southland. He was an "Okie" who'd come west during the Dust Bowl years with his parents; both his birthplace and the dark hue of his skin made him unwelcome in most parts of the City of Angels.

Gordon knew racism, too. Among other things, he and several black musicians had been invited to play at Hollywood clubs where African American audiences weren't allowed in to see them. Gordon's interest in music was a longstanding one. His father, a doctor, had treated Duke Ellington, Lionel Hampton, and other jazz stars on their California tours. Now all Los Angeles believed Dexter Gordon was the strongest player of the present generation.

Gordon and Gray had met before. Both men had toured with big bands in the East before turning their fingers to be-bop, a new kind of jazz jumping up from the streets. They'd run into each other in Detroit years back. And, only a few weeks before, they'd both stood in line in this very same room to pay homage to a visitor, the famous alto sax player Charlie Parker. But tonight the two were here to compete.

Gordon assembled his saxophone in full view of the crowded tables below, polishing the neck of the horn with a rag as he made sure all eyes in the place were on him. He blew a few testing notes, then signaled to the boys on the side. The band picked up the beat, then dropped its volume to let the soloist take over.

Sweet and powerful, that's what Gordon's sound was. He followed the melody at first, then began to play a kind of music that jumped here and there with an underlying reason. His rhythm set the standard: "I'm still here," it said. "I'm the best." When he had finished, the local favorite stepped back to await the crowd's reaction.

Right away, skinny Wardell Gray slid forward, looking like a gust of wind might blow him over. But instead, the Thin Man blew air into his long saxophone and surprised the unofficial "judges." He played fast, light, and sure. The melody came out straight, then curled and twirled. After his minute of song, Gray ended with a little jab that, to the listeners below, seemed as sweet as dessert.

Then it was Gordon's turn again, his chance to show off. Taking command, he decided to lay down new chord changes, moving the music in colorful leaps and bounds. His was a show of virtuosity and perfect tone. As soon as Gordon finished, Gray came forward and did just the opposite: he stuck tight to the standard notes. But he made the melody's clouds fill the room. Even the band behind him couldn't help but be impressed.

The two men dueled again and again as the band kept pace. First went Gordon with pulse and beauty, followed by soft-spoken Gray with lilt and a line. They played for shorter and shorter periods, so that after a few minutes they were tossing what seemed like musical sentences back and forth. Then just phrases, then words, then one or two potent notes. Call and response, run and follow, Gordon's drive chased by Gray's sigh. At last the two played loud and together, and the whole audience burst into applause.

Who had won the title of musical heavyweight? Which style was better, the boxer's or the butterfly's? Sweaty and full of adrenaline, the two tenor players shook hands and smiled as the crowd debated. Each listener had heard something different, and each scored it in his or her own way. But everyone in The Bird in the Basket agreed on one thing: they'd never seen a match like it. Word filtered up to the musicians at last. The musical duet was a dead heat. The winner, someone declared, was the audience.

A month later, the two tenor sax players met again, this time in a Hollywood recording studio. Their 78-rpm record of "The Chase," made on June 12, 1947, broke all sales expectations; it was the best-selling title in the nation. And it preserved Dexter Gordon's and Wardell Gray's complementary styles for all jazz history.

1952

California Cuisine

The mini golden cheese-filled tortillas—*quesadillas,* the locals called them—steamed in the warm evening air as the cook placed them on her flower-laden table. "You can eat these with your fingers once they cool," she explained. "And dip them in that tomato salsa, if you'd like."

"What's inside?" one of her dinner guests asked.

"Monterey Jack cheese," Helen Brown answered, "one of California's best inventions."

For the late summer dinner, the exuberant cook had moved the dining table to the patio where her guests, visiting from the East, might enjoy the best part of the day. Alongside the flowers and a scattering of pearly shells, Helen set down a colorful assortment of good things to eat, dish after dish. Near a molded guacamole aspic she placed a huge green salad flavored with such tasty treats as walnut oil, pomegranate seeds, and edible nasturtiums. From the kitchen, she brought forth a grilled breast of chicken garnished with lemon and herbs.

"Wine, anyone?" she asked. "It's white California wine, of course—a dry Semillon. Nothing could be better."

Helen Brown's eastern visitors may not have known what to make of the food and the intoxicating atmosphere, but they certainly enjoyed it. Compared to the meat-and-potatoes fare they were used to, Helen's fresh menu seemed like something foreign, possibly Mediterranean. But their host swore that her food was completely American, and that every dish came from the West Coast and its many cultures. They were eating locally. Helen called it California cuisine.

To some who lived in postwar California, food was a metaphor for the region's possibilities. The fabulous fifties brought optimism to many Californians, as national prosperity opened the door to new ideas. Middle-class people could afford to experiment with new and exotic ingredients. Housewives sent back home after wartime work were seeking new experiences. For those with energy and curiosity, each meal could be a miniature event.

Every meal at Helen Brown's house certainly was. Helen was the new California cuisine's best missionary. She had cooked up West Coast dinners for many friends, testing out the area's best recipes. With her husband Philip she traveled up and down the coast to find new ingredients and cooking techniques. Drawn to the Spanish dishes that called up the ghosts of the missions, Helen traveled south to Ensenada, Mexico. When she'd had enough chocolate and chilies, she headed north to San Francisco's Chinatown and learned how to fold wontons. A meal at Helen's was never dull.

As she cleared the dinner plates from the patio table, Helen reminded her guests that California was the grocery basket of the nation. Fruits and vegetables could be picked there year-round, and the Pacific Ocean was full of shellfish and tuna. California's past had been a cavalcade of cultures, each with its own specialty foods. Helen had spent many hours in her large kitchen learning about California's culinary offerings and experimenting with fresh-ground spices and offbeat ingredients.

The Browns had come west twenty years earlier from New England, where Helen had worked in the restaurant business. The slim, dark-haired woman sensed almost instinctively which foods went well together and which stood best alone. As she served dessert—a fancy pastry like those she made for a local bakery—Helen looked up to see her handiwork complemented by a sugary pink sunset. Her guests went off into the night well-fed and smiling.

It wasn't long before Helen Brown decided to share her love of California cookery with a wider audience. She and Philip compiled her regional recipes for a small publishing house in 1952. Helen's *West Coast Cook Book* brought the tastes of California to the nation and gave the Pasadena cook an opportunity to entertain famous guests, including the great American chef James Beard, who showed up on her doorstep.

California cuisine is still with us today, more popular than ever as the Locavore movement has taken hold. Using fresh ingredients in unique combinations remains one of California's best ideas, the perfect symbol of a state that prides itself on variety.

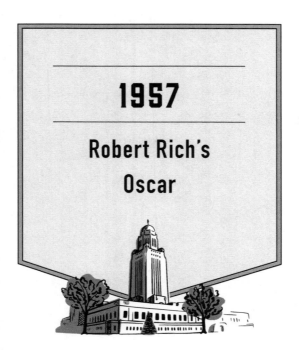

1957

Robert Rich's Oscar

The competition for best screenplay was a lock: the trophy was sure to go to the writer of *The Brave One,* a movie shaped by themes of courage and alienation. Members of the Academy of Motion Picture Arts and Sciences had voted by secret ballot, and one of the gold statuettes known as an Oscar waited for the best screenwriter to claim it. "And the winner is . . . ," the presenter drawled into the microphone, pausing to open the sealed envelope with the results of the vote, ". . . Robert Rich."

The crowd applauded, but the writer did not appear on stage to claim his due. Instead, the Academy accepted the award for him. Its award show organizers knew what many in the audience did not: that the man named Robert Rich didn't exist.

The person who had earned the award was home with his family, watching the ceremony on television. Dalton Trumbo was a fifty-two-year-old writer, one of Hollywood's most talented pens. The author of a pacifist novel, *Johnny Got His Gun,* Trumbo had turned to screen work for the income. Writing for the movies was a job you could do in the bathtub, he liked to say. He proved it by churning out scripts from just such a place, among them *The Defiant Ones* and *Lonely Are the Brave.*

Dalton Trumbo's work was now done in secret, though, and submitted under one of twelve different false names, one of which was Robert Rich. There was a reason for the intrigue. Dalton Trumbo was on the blacklist.

After World War II, California fostered an atmosphere of fear and patriotism. Although fascist governments had been defeated in the war, many people perceived a new threat coming from Russia in the form of communism. University professors and others of influence were asked to sign loyalty oaths to the state and nation. The Russians were coming— or so Senator Joseph McCarthy had implied. Some people turned paranoid, believing that Stalin's Reds were everywhere, especially in loose, liberal Los Angeles. Neighbors and even friends could not be trusted.

McCarthy's accusations had prompted the formation of fact-finding committees such as the one run by Jack Tenney in the California legislature and the House Un-American Activities Committee in Congress. HUAC, as it was called, brought suspected symphathizers to the stand and asked the famous question, "Are you now or have you ever been a member of the Communist Party?" Those who said yes could clear themselves in only one way—by helping the investigators ferret out fellow Communists, or "pinkos" as they called them.

Congress peered hardest at the entertainment industry. Communist writers and directors, it said, could influence innocent minds through the movies. It began a witch hunt for card-carrying Reds in the Hollywood ranks. At first, none of the filmmakers would testify. But a few buckled under the pressure—or the desire to get rid of competitors. "Friendly" witnesses named names. Among those they listed was Dalton Trumbo.

Like so many others in the 1930s, Trumbo was an idealist who had believed in the new Soviet Union. He had not advocated violent overthrow of the U.S. government or anything else even remotely traitorous. As his early writings showed, he was for peace at any cost.

But HUAC was a three-ring circus with full Congressional powers. After a shouting match with the president of the Screen Writer's Guild, the committee put ten of Hollywood's brightest in federal prison for refusing to answer their questions. Behind bars went directors Herbert Biberman and Edward Dmytryk along with writers Alvah Bessie, Lester Cole, Ring Lardner Jr., John Howard Lawson, Albert Maltz, Samuel Ornitz, Adrian Scott, and Dalton Trumbo.

The publicity terrified studio heads, who feared that HUAC would go even further and start to censor their casting choices. To avoid any uncertainty, they did it themselves. Suspected Reds and pinkos were put on a blacklist, and the leaders of the movie business agreed that no one was to hire them.

The "Hollywood Ten" had not been convicted of any crime other than contempt of HUAC's methods. But their careers were shot down anyway. Some of the blacklisted writers went to Europe or Canada, where they could still find jobs. Others, including Trumbo, refused to cower. They headed back to Hollywood and made up false identities or borrowed the names of non-blacklisted writers to keep working in film.

It was not easy for their families, especially their children, who could not pretend to be who they weren't. School administrators took away an award for academic achievement they had given to Chris Trumbo, Dalton's son, after they discovered who his father was.

The sham Academy Award presentation of 1957 topped it all. The prestigious Academy would not admit that one of the blacklisted writers deserved a golden Oscar. The ceremony's producer covered for the missing Robert Rich by saying he was traveling in Spain. The fantasy makers then went to work in earnest: they got *Life* magazine to run a profile on the imaginary Rich, a shy, solitary traveler who wrote film scripts. They kept up the charade for two years.

By 1959, the Cold War blacklist had gone a little gray, and Dalton Trumbo was one of the first writers to see his name back in the credits of new films. Getting rid of the old false identities was another story. It took Trumbo nearly twenty years to get official credit for his Oscar. Other writers had to wait even longer to get the recognition they deserved. Not until 1996 did Sony Pictures put blacklisted writer Michael Wilson's name on the prints of his picture *Lawrence of Arabia*. Wilson didn't live to see it happen.

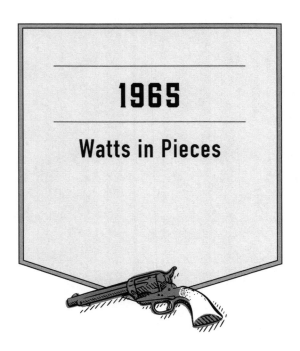

1965

Watts in Pieces

On a hot Wednesday night in August 1965, on the outskirts of the community of Watts, an officer of the Los Angeles Police Department (LAPD) pulled over a Buick he thought had been weaving drunkenly. Inside were two young African American men who protested their innocence to the white officer. Their mother soon arrived on the scene and began to add her vocal opinion: her sons had borrowed her car without asking.

It was still early evening—not yet seven o'clock—and the fuss drew a crowd. The young men got bolder with an audience, and the white officer got more wary and militant. His single billy club was no help against the number of onlookers, now laughing and yelling. "Code 1199," he radioed. "Officer Needs Assistance." When backup police arrived on the scene, they clubbed and pushed the two young men, their mother, and a woman bystander from a nearby beauty parlor into squad cars and took them away.

The LAPD had seldom been gentle with the people of Los Angeles's largest black neighborhood. The crowd agreed that this time their pushy disrespect had gone too far. More people gathered, and within an hour a thousand angry residents had gathered in the streets. They threw rocks at police cars that circled the area. Later, they brought out guns. Watts disintegrated into a full-scale riot.

Watts had seemed an unlikely place for mayhem and burning. On the outside, it looked like a typical California enclave of stucco houses surrounding a business district. Its streets were wide and lined with lawns and single-family homes. But beyond the obvious lay a fearsome frustration.

For African American citizens in California, life had not lived up to its promises. They were the last hired and first laid off in most regional industries. The City of Los Angeles had made the problem worse by allowing open discrimination in housing laws and social services. The nearly one thousand people who moved to Watts and other parts of south-central Los Angeles each month found increasingly cramped conditions and poor transportation. The new freeway systems were of little use to people without cars, and city bus routes were outdated and insufficient. Watts had slipped into ghetto status. Its people saw no clear way to fight the trend.

Most of the new arrivals were young men who had come from small towns in the South. They were used to various forms of racism and were especially wary of policemen since, in the 1960s, law enforcement rarely came down on their side. The LAPD had done nothing to win them over. It treated blacks more harshly than it treated whites, every time. Chief of Police William Parker had only to open his mouth and out flew racist comments.

On that particular August night, however, the arrest of four of their own people caused the neighbors of Watts to lash back. The Watts-Willowbrook area glowed with a pent-up fury. One in every six residents picked up a weapon, and double that number became active spectators. Rioters ran through the streets, sabotaging police efforts at control. Stores were ransacked. The LAPD thought the stores were being hit in a random pattern, but for the most part the looters targeted businesses that had charged more than the going rate, or had cared little for the neighborhood: pawn shops, liquor stores, clothing sellers. There was also racism on the part of the Watts rioters, who hit Korean store owners particularly hard.

After two days of broken glass and fighting, the rioters began to burn entire blocks. The riot zone expanded to an area fifty or sixty streets wide, encompassing more than four hundred square miles. The police could not contain it. Outside the ghetto, California's white, Latino, and Asian populations watched the news in fear for their lives. The acting governor decided to send in the National Guard.

By that time, the violence had begun to take a toll. Ambulance crews had to brave sniper fire to pick up wounded people. Residents of the community tried to convince family members to stop what they were doing and come inside where they could be safe. Some did, but others stayed on the rampage for four more days. The National Guard pushed through with shields and guns, and on Tuesday, August 18, nearly a week after it had started, the riot collapsed.

Thirty-four African Americans were dead, more than a thousand people were wounded, and nearly four thousand had been arrested. Watts looked as though it had been struck by an earthquake.

The people of Watts tried to pick up the pieces but found their whole lives were made of bits of brick and broken glass, like the quirky Watts Towers made by an Italian immigrant, Sabato Rodia. The city had been forced to listen in the worst kind of way, but did it understand? Police Chief Parker would not admit that race relations had had anything to do with the violence. It was just a hot night, he said, and tempers had gone wild. Nothing would change; nothing had been solved.

Although the African Americans of Los Angeles were able to claim more of their civil rights as the 1960s marched on, they still had grievances and a desire for change. More than twenty-five years after Watts burned the first time, the arrest and beating of an African American named Rodney King, again by the LAPD, would trigger another equally horrible scene of destruction.

1966

Cruising the Freeways

At the sound of the alarm clock, Marilee Farrier got up from the small motor home's bed to feed her baby. Once the child was content, Marilee started the engine of her home, drove it from its nightly parking spot to the Hollywood Freeway, and headed east toward the Cahuenga exit. Her husband Steve slept most of the way; he was between shifts. He woke in time to have breakfast before Marilee dropped him off at work. They were a family, after all, and mealtimes were sacred.

Marilee kept driving, all the way to San Bernardino, where she dropped off the baby at her mother's house and continued on to work herself. Marilee's mother was a gracious grandma. She didn't mind keeping an eye on the little one while the young parents tried to improve their circumstances.

The Farriers had come to Los Angeles from Seattle, and originally had settled into a typical California existence. They bought a home in Tujunga Canyon and spent Saturdays and Sundays camping. After a few years of prosperity, they took out a loan to purchase a motor home and enjoyed more weekend jaunts. Then the impossible thing happened: both of them lost their jobs.

The Farriers could find no way to pay off their debts. The highest bills were the payments on their house, car, and motor home. At that point they saw the light: why keep both a home and a car, when the motor home could serve both needs? The Farriers agreed that until they could save up some money, they would live in their Winnebago, sleeping at night and cruising the freeways of Southern California's megalopolis by day.

Marilee made the run to San Bernardino each morning, then drove back to downtown Los Angeles each night. Steve worked two jobs. One of his employers owned a building with a secured, well-lit parking lot. Here the couple parked each night before bedtime. The situation was not the best, but it was manageable. The Farriers covered about 128 miles each day, on ten gallons of gas. "If you figure twenty-two working days, that means we spend about seventy-five dollars a month on commuting, which really isn't so bad," Steve said. It certainly was cheaper than owning a home and operating a car on the spiderweb of Los Angeles County roads.

America in the mid-1960s was a place of miracles. Technology had made it possible for a family to live its entire life on the freeway. Possible, but not probable. In fact, the whole story of the Farriers was a hoax. William Bronson and the editors at *Cry California,* an environmental journal, published the piece in 1966 to illustrate the essential pointlessness of California's car culture.

What Bronson hadn't made up was the impact the Cal-Trans freeway system was having on Southern California and its citizens. In a city with no efficient mass transportation, most people drove to get where they were going—some starting their engines to travel only a few blocks. The automotive industry did provide economic benefits, of course. Nearly half a million Californians were employed in jobs directly related to cars. Thousands of people worked in automotive finance or insurance, to say nothing of the medical services each traffic accident required. But the costs of a car-dominated culture were high, too: smog, dwindling petroleum supplies, global warming, frayed nerves. Some commuters actually spent as many hours on the road each day as did the fictional Farriers.

The environmentalists' satire bit hard, but it did not change things. Southern Californians loved their cars. Some even craved the sense of freedom they got within their glass and steel pods, cruising the freeways just for the thrill of it. More than 22 million licensed drivers in California today travel 271 billion miles each year. The story of the couple who lived on the freeways had turned into an urban myth, one that still circulates among motorists as they navigate their 35 million vehicles on the state's complex network of roads.

1969

Surveillance Video

The man in the pinstriped suit bent over sideways, peering into the television monitor. He leaned so far he nearly lost his balance. The picture on the screen made no sense to him. It showed the very same corridor in which he was standing, but it did not show his image. He wasn't there. He could see where the camera was mounted, and could watch the monitor from all points as he moved down the hall, but the camera never picked him up—it showed only empty space. The Los Angeles art scene, especially the Nicholas Wilder Gallery, had finally taken minimalism too far, he thought. A hallway with a camera that didn't seem to work properly was not his kind of art.

In fact, the installation with the apparently broken camera was an art form that very few people in California knew about: video art. It was an art form that would change the way people looked at television, and at their world.

The video artist who had set up the surveillance camera was Bruce Nauman. He had built the piece, called *Corridor,* in order to challenge Californians' perceptions. The work, set up in the hallway of Wilder's gallery, was one of the earliest exhibitions of video art in the country; it helped establish videotape as a new creative medium. Nauman first designed and built a special narrow hall and placed a video monitor at its end. He then added a surveillance camera that pointed at anyone who looked into the narrow slot between the two walls. Viewers expected to see themselves on the monitor, which showed pictures of what seemed to be the same hallway. But Nauman was more clever than that. Instead of displaying what the surveillance camera picked up, he played a tape loop of an empty hallway. He then watched as visitors danced and bent sideways trying to find themselves onscreen.

Nauman was interested in the fact that, by 1969, all America was glued to the curved sheet of glass called TV. His sample of the new video art commented on this TV culture. Television had begun as a kind of radio with pictures, where announcers read news from white sheets of paper. Soon the television networks developed variety acts and quiz shows to keep people entertained. The programming was bland, and friendly. It was the perfect arena for situation comedies sponsored by advertisers of domestic products.

As an artist, Nauman experimented with different mediums. He also wondered what the future of television would hold. Would it stick to the basics, or could it be used in unexplored, innovative ways? From the start, television's producers were linked to the Los Angeles Basin. The kind of programming they needed was easy to film in Hollywood, a land of sets and studios. The little community of Burbank, just northeast of the film center, became television's hometown.

Events in Southern California and the world also shaped Nauman's views of the new technology. In the late 1960s, TV was used to report live news of the war in Vietnam. For the first time, home viewers could see graphic, violent images on the blue screen's glowing face. Americans watched battle scenes and the signs of horrific acts of chemical warfare from their living rooms. The technology slimmed down, and became portable, so that video could be made in all corners of the globe. The invention of the Sony Portapak, a video camera that anyone could carry and use, brought video into reach as an art form. Easily shot, and easily edited, it was the quintessential observer.

Nauman knew that we would soon be watching television watch us. The reactions of the audience at the Nicholas Wilder Gallery were an essential part of his installation. The viewers' gyrations to the mismatched video called attention to television's potential manipulation of reality. Video images, which seemed to be perfectly real, could be altered to reflect an alternate reality. In Nauman's view, this meant that even news video could be changed and edited. In the new world of global media, viewers might bend from side to side and still not get the entire picture.

1988

The Condor Puppet Show

In one of the sterile back rooms at the Los Angeles Zoo, a young biologist rolled up the sleeve of her lab coat and pulled a pink puppet over her hand. The fabric, painted with a bird's beak and eyes, stretched nearly to her shoulder. If the zoo scientist felt silly at first, she soon grew serious at her task. The "puppet show" for which she had dressed would not be performed for a crowd of kindergartners. Instead, it would have a rare and endangered audience: one of the first California condors to be hatched in captivity. Transformed by the painted cloth and a black curtain, the young woman would play the part of the baby bird's mother.

Only a short time before, ecstatic biologists had spread the word: a baby California condor had cracked its hard eggshell and struggled free. Newborn condors make an astounding effort to hatch. They come into the world exhausted, but they can still see and hear things that are close by. In Los Angeles and at San Diego's Wild Animal Park, where a similar experiment was in progress, keepers had to feed the chicks by placing the food deep in their throats. This posed a problem. The young birds were meant for a future in the wild, and they could not be allowed to develop a relationship with humans. These chicks had to learn a condor way of life, not a human one.

The dedicated biologists found a solution—the condor puppet show. Each person feeding a condor chick covered his or her arm with a long piece of fabric painted to look like an adult bird. The keepers fed the downy chicks from behind a black curtain so that the young birds would believe their condor parents kept them alive.

Condors were true symbols of the wild. The largest birds in North America, these black-bodied vultures with ten-foot wingspans had lived in California for forty thousand years, longer than humans had. They were bald-headed scavengers. Among their favorite foods were carcasses of fish and seals along the Pacific cliffs and beaches. The Chumash Indians had called the dark birds with white wing marks "thunderbirds" and built religious ceremonies around them. They had cast shadows on the hills for a very long time.

But the historic giants of the California skies had nearly died out. California's early settlers killed condors that stopped to feed on dead calves or trash piles. Once the region's coast was hemmed in by piers, bungalows, and large commercial harbors, the birds' main food source was gone. Shy and wary, they did not like people and moved inland to the roughest stretches of the Tehachapi and San Gabriel

Mountains. In more recent times, power lines and bullets had taken their toll. Pesticide residues weakened the birds' eggs, and California condors died faster than they could reproduce. By 1986, there were only twenty-one left in the world.

The Condor Recovery Team had been organized to save the endangered birds. The scientists' goal was to protect all the mature condors they could find. Condors do not begin to breed until they are six years old and normally lay only one egg every other year thereafter. The biologists captured the last breeding pair in the wild and brought it and other birds into large enclosed areas they called "condorminiums." These screened cages would serve as a controlled environment and might help the birds to breed.

In order to get the captive condors to lay as many eggs as possible, the recovery team removed each bluish, five-inch gem from the nest as soon as it was laid. The biologists had to incubate the eggs themselves, keeping them warm and turning them several times each day, as the wild birds did, to prevent the chicks from sticking to one side of the shell. Once hatched, the young birds represented the first good chance that condors might once again soar and circle above the Southland, saved from extinction.

The puppeteers raised their chicks well. By 1991, the Condor Recovery Team felt confident enough to release condors back into the Sespe Condor Sanctuary near Fillmore. The condor population in both zoos and mountains had begun to rally. Today more than a hundred condors fly free over Southern California's wild places, most successfully at Big Sur, and more have been released in Arizona, near the Vermilion Cliffs. In all, more than three hundred thunderbirds await their chance to soar in the wind.

1996

Saving Malibu

Flames slithered, snakelike, up and sideways with the wind. Each breeze fed oxygen to the fire, which crackled in the late autumn heat. Amid the blistered stems of oak scrub, Los Angeles County firefighters unrolled hoses and handed out shovels. "Wet down your yard, then clear the area!" one of them shouted to a woman who stood, hose in hand, on the roof of her home. "You're in danger if the flames turn this way, ma'am!"

"I'm not leaving," the red-haired actress yelled down from her perch. "I'm staying to fight!"

"Just so you know the danger," the firefighter responded.

"We all know the danger," the woman shouted back. "We live here, don't we?"

Alongside other residents of the hills and draws that make up the area called Malibu, Shirley MacLaine watched as the blue smoke rose nearby. Her home was threatened, and she was not about to leave without doing all she could to keep it from burning.

Professional firefighters said that staying in the area was foolhardy; the fire line was a dangerous place to be. October's unrelieved heat had left the coastal chaparral at its most delicate. Pale grass and dusty twigs snapped underfoot, brittle and dry. Anything could have started the blaze—even sunlight filtered through a broken bottle. The slightest glow could spark an inferno in those conditions. Fire burned hot in such an atmosphere, jumping easily from branch to branch. It could flash across tens of yards in seconds.

The City of Malibu had set up crisis centers and shelters, and most area residents had gone into Los Angeles to stay with friends for the duration. But other people in the area stayed at their posts to the end. Movie stars, business owners, or students, they knew that by choosing to live here they were part of a natural drama. MacLaine and the others swept their yards clean of dead grass and tinder. They filled empty tubs and buckets with water for use as a last resort. They turned on hoses and sprinkler systems to keep walls and shingles damp and fire-resistant. As helicopters carrying flame retardant buzzed overhead, small as bees in the giant arc of the sky, the people on the ground felt their emotions fan and flag. How could they let their homes—their lives—go up in smoke? The fire could take all they had at any moment.

After days of anxious watching, good news arrived. The fire had been stopped at the top of a ridgeline. Ten homes and more than a thousand acres were charred, but no lives had been lost. Morning fog shrouded the embers as Malibu celebrated. The little town and its surroundings had been saved—again.

The fire of 1996 was not the first to singe Malibu's green hills, and it was not the last. In fact, the area burns at some level almost annually, flaring notably in 1956 when one man died and seventy-two houses turned to ash, and in 2007 and 2008, when more than a million acres of Los Angeles, Orange, Riverside, Santa Barbara, and San Diego counties went up in flame. Hundreds of homes were lost. The same thorny little scrub oaks, chamisas, and canyon laurels that make the seaside hills beautiful also make ideal fuel. Unlike most plant communities, the chaparral does most of its growing in winter. In autumn, the green leaves of the oaks shrink and turn red-brown as they wait for the rains to begin. After the drying November winds, showers come, as historian Carey McWilliams wrote, "drifting in long graceful veils, washing the land, clearing the atmosphere: the gentlest baptism imaginable." Chaparral is a miracle carpet that burns and recovers.

But homes and businesses do not grow back without a great deal of human effort. It does not take a crystal ball to see that, in such an environment, disaster inevitably will strike again. Fire at Malibu is an event that repeats, a reminder that the land was here long before we were, and that it follows its own predictable cycles. The hills and canyons of Malibu will burn, over and over. And Southern Californians will build there again, beginning yet another episode in the Southland's history.

2003

The Governator

As the summer of 2003 dragged on into dusty fall, the Southland grew desperate. Its economy had crashed, sent toward the floor by a bust in the state's tech industries and "dot coms." California Governor Gray Davis had mismanaged funds and left the state in arrears. His government was inefficient, and the state legislature couldn't come up with so much as a budget for the year to come. To make it worse, a dry heat simmered in the region, and the ubiquitous air conditioners were of little help in most households. Power was scarce—there were rolling blackouts, due to shortages, and electricity prices soared to three times what they had been the year before.

Californians couldn't help but sweat and swear. If only they had a hero to save them from the state's collapsing infrastructure! If only a robotic man from the future would appear to straighten out the mess!

Enter Arnold Schwarzenegger.

An Austrian immigrant who had come to the United States as a young bodybuilder, Schwarzenegger was one of America's top action film heroes. His beefy physique had earned him the title of Mr. Universe and the nickname "The Austrian Oak." As Mr. Olympia, an honor he won seven times, he tuned his body to the ultimate combination of muscle and sinew. He was obsessed, by his own admission, with lifting weights, but he envisioned a better career and determined to make his way in Hollywood.

Starring in several science fiction movies, he was a little known character actor before his fame overcame his thick European accent. Schwarzenegger was always the most powerful man in the cast, known for his brawn and good humor. *The Terminator* was his most famous film; in 2003, his third version of the story, *Terminator 2: 3D,* had filled California movie screens.

At the time, what the state of California needed in its political arena was someone just like Arnold's onscreen characters—someone tough, who could prompt the legislature into action. Governor Gray Davis had dried up, most agreed, and he was paralyzed by his own bad decisions. Since 1911, Californians had had the right to recall their elected officials if they didn't pass muster. They had tried to do so 117 times but had never succeeded. Still, interested parties thought the time had come. They called for new leadership, signed petitions, submitted forms, and the recall election was set.

Top candidates for a new governor included the current Lieutenant Governor Cruz Bustamante, who broke with his boss. Also running were Republican State Senator Tom McClintock and independent political maven Arianna Huffington. The field of more than one hundred gubernatorial wannabes also included some odd choices: onetime baseball commissioner Peter Ueberroth, former child star Gary Coleman, and porn star Mary Carey Cook. No one candidate seemed to take hold, and the ever unraveling string of possibilities became a huge joke. One television network even held a game show called *Who Wants to be Governor of California?* Comedian Jay Leno suggested that Arnold Schwarzenegger might be best in such a *"Total Recall"* election, which hinted at the name of one of Arnold's action films. No one really expected the movie star to run for governor.

What they had not figured on was Schwarzenegger's family history and his own political ambitions. The child of a former Nazi policeman, raised harshly in hard times, Schwarzenegger had a difficult youth. He had always been inspired by American democracy and how it offered individuals a chance to thrive. When he came to this country in 1968 at age 21, he had nothing but determination. One of the first things he witnessed was a presidential debate between California's son Richard Nixon and Democrat Hubert Humphrey. "A friend of mine who spoke German and English translated for me," Schwarzenegger later remembered. "I heard Nixon speak. He was talking about free enterprise, getting the government off your back, lowering the taxes and strengthening the military. Listening to Nixon speak sounded more like a breath of fresh air." The Austrian joined the Republican party when he became a U.S. citizen in 1983.

Schwarzenegger was a businessman, too, a millionaire in the mail order and bricklaying businesses before he was ever a film star. His free market values were tempered by his affability and centrist nature. He married into a Democratic political dynasty when he married President John F. Kennedy's niece Maria Shriver. Though he had supported George H. W. Bush for president, he had environmental leanings. He could be forceful, but he also knew how to talk to people and convince them to work in their own best interests. As a celebrity, he brought a bit of sparkle to the fray.

He announced his candidacy on Leno's *Tonight Show,* and the race was on. The election played out in the media, and why not? Californians loved drama. At a debate on September 24 between the top five candidates at Cal State Sacramento, large crowds gathered like those at a movie premiere. Schwarzenegger and his peers made their way down a long, red carpet to a dais under the glow of golden lights. More than five hundred reporters and cameramen watched the debate, sending images around the globe. Some of them represented hard news organizations; others were from the fluff networks such as *E!* or *Entertainment Tonight.* The film star came out best in front of the cameras. On the following day, both Arianna Huffington and Peter Ueberroth pulled out of the race.

Two weeks later, on October 7, 2003, California voters went to the polls. The first question on the ballot was whether or not they wished to recall Gray Davis and replace him. They voted yes, overwhelmingly. The second question was tougher. With whom should they replace him? As Californians cast their votes, the media circled with lights and cameras, waiting for the final tallies. By ten o'clock that night, Governor Davis conceded to the action hero. A majority of California residents—4,206,284 voters—had said the governor should go, and Schwarzenegger had won his seat by a plurality. The voters had given their new Governator more votes than his three closest competitors combined. Schwarzenegger accepted their decision humbly, saying, "Today California has given me the greatest gift of all. You've given me your trust by voting for me. I will do everything I can to live up to that trust. I will not fail you." Schwarzenegger was the first foreign-born governor of California since Irishman John G. Downey held the post in 1862.

Schwarzenegger's first year on the job wasn't easy. He couldn't go into the legislative chambers like a soldier in camouflage or a robot hit man. He had to convince politicians and lifelong bureaucrats that he could work with them, partly on their terms. He donated his annual salary of $175,000 to charity. He worked from his own home in the Brentwood section of Los Angeles, choosing to live in the Hyatt Regency Hotel in Sacramento when the legislature required his presence. A few clouds of scandal hovered over the halls of government—Arnold called his opponents "girlie men" and was accused himself of being a ladies' man and possible harasser. Yet he also got the job done. "I saw that people, not just in California, but across the nation, were hungry for a new kind of politics," he said, "a politics that looks beyond the old labels, the old ways, the old arguments."

As governor, Schwarzenegger repealed various licensing fees and fought against gridlock. He strengthened copyright law and enacted many types of environmental legislation. Utility emissions, greenhouse gases, and other factors in global warming became his new enemies. Criticized for driving gas-guzzling Hummers, Schwarzenegger altered one of his fleet to run on hydrogen and another to burn biodiesel.

He even saved a drowning tourist in Hawaii while he was there on vacation. His efforts earned him the nickname "The People's Governor." In November 2006 he won reelection over Phil Angelides by a tremendous margin—more people voted for him than had the first time, and he won by more than a million votes. With term limits, the Governor would stay in office only through 2010, and after the struggles of state economic failure in 2009 that may have been just fine with him.

Life as an action hero hasn't been easy. California's action hero has lived through motorcycle crashes, heart surgery, and a broken leg in his Sacramento seasons. The fiscal crisis the nation faced in 2009–2010 was perhaps the most difficult of these. When times got tough, the governor could review what his persistent character in *The Terminator* did in the face of destruction. Schwarzenegger and the nation will be able to view the film for a long time to come—in 2008, the Library of Congress announced that it would be one of only twenty-five films added to the National Film Registry.

SOUTHERN CALIFORNIA/ HOLLYWOOD/SILVER SCREEN FACTS AND TRIVIA

- California is the third largest state, bigger than 85 of the world's smallest nations put together. It measures 158,693 square miles, or 101,563,520 acres.

- California was the name of a fictional island in *Las Sergas de Esplandían,* a romance by the Spanish writer García Ordóñez de Montalvo, published in 1510. The name was given to what is now Baja California by the Spanish explorers Hernando Cortes and Fortún Ximenez early in the sixteenth century.

- California's shoreline is so long that it would reach from Boston, Massachusetts, to Charleston, South Carolina.

- In 1962, California became the most populous state in the union, with more than 22 million residents. Today it is home to more than 36,457,000 people, with more than 217 people per square mile.

- The "Golden State" was given its nickname because of the discovery of gold in 1848 at Sutter's Mill near Sacramento, today's state capital. But the name also reflects the California state flower, the golden poppy.

- Southern California deserts support seven hundred species of flowering plants, including blue lupines, yellow desert sunflowers, desert marigolds, sand verbena, and evening primroses.

- "I Love You, California," by F. B. Silverwood and A. F. Frankenstein, is the official state song.

- California's state bird, the California valley quail, lives in dry scrub and canyons. It cannot be found in the thick groves of California redwood, which is the state tree.

- Its drivers commute an average of 28 minutes to work or school.

- Californians use more than 35,100,000,000 gallons of fresh water per day.

- Three out of four days in California are sunny.

- California's lowest temperature on record was -45 degrees F on January 20, 1937 at Boca, elevation 5,532 feet. The temperature at Greenland Ranch, 178 feet below sea level, reached 134 degrees F on July 10, 1913, also a record.

- California is one of the most urban states in the country. Only New Jersey, Rhode Island, Connecticut, Massachusetts, and Maryland have more metropolitan areas per capita.

- The average Californian is 32 years old, is white or Latino, female, and lives in the Los Angeles Basin.

- Any U.S. citizen who lives in California and is 18 years old is eligible to run for governor or any other elected state office.

- The first movie studio in Hollywood was the Nestor Studio, which opened in October 1911.

- The Los Angeles *Times* is the fourth largest newspaper in the United States, with a morning circulation of 1,089,690. The San Francisco *Chronicle* ranks tenth.

- Southern California supplies all of the U.S.'s and most of the western world's requirements for boron and borax, used in many manufactured items including cardboard, toothpaste, and laundry detergent.

- The first feature film made in Hollywood was in 1914 and was called *The Squaw Man*. It was directed by Cecil B. DeMille (who would make many epic films over the years) and Oscar Apfel.

- DeMille filmed *The Squaw Man* three different times: in 1914, 1918, and 1931.

- In his career, D. W. Griffith made almost 500 films (many, however, just brief-ten minute productions).

- The first film to be shown in the White House was Griffith's *The Birth of a Nation,* in 1915, for President Woodrow Wilson.

- The huge wall of Babylon set, which D.W. Griffith had built for the film *Intolerance,* stood at the corner of Hollywood and Sunset Boulevards for four years. It was eventually declared a fire hazard and was torn down in 1919.

- For authenticity in filming sequences at the end of the modern story in *Intolerance,* Griffith used the services of Martin Aguerre, a former warden of Sing Sing Prison. Aguerre supervised the building of a gallows for the execution scene.

- Charlie Chaplin was the first actor to appear on the cover of *Time* magazine (July 6, 1925).

- Charlie Chaplin was knighted at Buckingham Palace, just three miles from the slums where he grew up.

- Actress Mabel Normand was once a professional model and posed for such famous artists as Charles Dana and James Montgomery Flagg.

- The first person to leave prints in the cement in front of Grauman's Chinese Theatre was actress Norma Talmadge, who accidentally stepped into newly laid cement. From this a tradition was started.

- Both Walt Disney and Ernest Hemingway worked for the *Kansas City Star*—Disney as an artist, Hemingway as a reporter.

- Even though the Academy Awards were first presented in 1927, the first native Californian to win for best actor was Gregory Peck for the film *To Kill a Mockingbird*—35 years later in 1962.

- Walt Disney holds the record for winning the most Academy Awards (26) and also the most nominations (64).

- When sound films were first proposed in the 1920s, studio boss Adolph Zukor was reported to have said, "The effect on the overseas market would be disastrous. Only a small part of the world speaks English."

- Although *The Jazz Singer* (1927) was the first feature film to use spoken dialogue, *Don Juan* (1926) was the first feature film with a soundtrack. The sound, however, was only a music score, performed by the 107-piece Philharmonic Orchestra, directed by Herman Heller.

- *The Jazz Singer* was the first feature film with spoken dialogue, but it has only two short dialogue scenes and the total spoken words number just 354.

- Sam Warner, one of the Warner Brothers, died on October 5, 1927, just one day before the release of *The Jazz Singer*, the film he had helped promote and which was the prime force in making their company into a major studio.

- *King Kong* (1933) was originally to be titled *The Beast*, then *The Eighth Wonder of the World*.

- Among the actresses considered for the lead in *King Kong* were Jean Harlow and Ginger Rogers. The role eventually went to Fay Wray.

- Two of the 18-inch models of Kong had to have their skins removed each day of filming so that the bolts and screws could be retightened.

- *King Kong* was the only movie to open simultaneously at both New York's Roxy Theater and Radio City Music Hall (just a few blocks away).

- Originally the New York appearance of the ape in *King Kong* was to take place in Yankee Stadium but was changed to a theater instead.

- Among the rejected names for dwarfs in Disney's *Snow White and the Seven Dwarfs* (1937) were: Jumpy, Hotsy, Shifty, Dirty, and Awful.

- At the 1937 Academy Awards, *Snow White and the Seven Dwarfs* received a special award: one full sized Oscar and seven small ones.

- The novel *Gone With the Wind* by Margaret Mitchell was turned down for film adaptation by almost every studio in Hollywood because of the expense to film it or because most studio bosses felt that "Civil War films don't make any money."

- The huge gates that had been used in *King Kong,* along with other old sets on the back lot of RKO Studios were set on fire as part of the "burning of Atlanta" scene in *Gone With the Wind.*

- Because of the Motion Picture Code, Rhett Butler's line, "Frankly, my dear, I don't give a damn" was also filmed as "Frankly, my dear, I don't care." The first choice, however, was eventually the one used.

- At the premiere of *Gone With the Wind* in Atlanta, Georgia, in 1939, black cast members were not permitted to attend due to the state's racial segregation laws.

- In addition to being the first film in which Orson Welles appeared, *Citizen Kane* also marked the film debuts of Joseph Cotten, Agnes Moorhead, and Ruth Warrick.

- Since William Randolph Hearst believed that *Citizen Kane* was directed at him and his life, newspapers run by the Hearst Company would not run advertising for the film.

- One of the most often quoted movie lines is "Play it again, Sam," in *Casablanca* (1942), but this line is never actually spoken in the film. Humphrey Bogart says, "Play it!" and Ingrid Bergman says, "Play it, Sam. Play 'As Time Goes By.' "

- As of 2009 only one family has produced three generations of Academy Award winners: the Hustons. John, best director for *The Treasure of the Sierra Madre* (1948), his father Walter for best supporting actor in the same film, and John's daughter Anjelica as Best Supporting Actress for *Prizzi's Honor* in 1985.

- The first commercial television station west of the Mississippi River was KTLA, and it began broadcasting in January 1947.

- The Hollywood Walk of Fame was created and the first star placed in 1958.

- Ub Iwerks, who worked for Walt Disney and who many believe was the real creator of Mickey Mouse, did the special effects for the 1963 Alfred Hitchcock film *The Birds*.

- Marilyn Monroe's real name was Norma Jeane Mortensen. Her mother supposedly named her for two famous actresses: Norma Talmadge and Jean Harlow.

- At an auction held by Christie's in New York, a pair of the "ruby slippers" worn by Judy Garland in *The Wizard of Oz* sold for $666,000.

- Hollywood does not have its own government (since it is part of Los Angeles), but it does have an "Honorary Mayor." This job was held for many years by TV personality Johnny Grant, until his death in 2008.

- In 2002 a campaign was begun to have Hollywood secede from Los Angeles and become a separate, incorporated municipality. The referendum was put on the ballot but failed by a wide margin.

- Studio boss Samuel Goldwyn was reputed to have said that a verbal contract "isn't worth the paper it's written on," and when once asked for his decision supposedly said, "I can give you a definite maybe."

- As of 2021 the film that has grossed more money than any other is *Avatar* (2009) with nearly three billion dollars earned internationally.

BIBLIOGRAPHY

Arnold, Caroline, and Michael Wallace. *On the Brink of Extinction: The California Condor.* San Diego and New York: Gulliver Green/Harcourt Brace Jovanovich, 1993.

Austin, Mary. *The Land of Little Rain.* 1903. Reprint. Albuquerque: University of New Mexico Press, 1974.

———. *Earth Horizon: Autobiography.* New York: The Literary Guild, 1932.

Bakker, Edna. *An Island Called California.* 2nd ed. Berkeley: University of California Press, 1984.

Belden, L. Burr. *Goodbye, Death Valley!: The Tragic 1849 Jayhawker Trek.* Death Valley '49ers Publication No. 5. Bishop, Calif.: Chalfant Press, 1956.

Biskind, Peter. *Seeing is Believing: How Hollywood Taught Us to Stop Worrying and Love the Fifties.* New York: Pantheon, 1983.

Brown, Helen Evans. *Helen Brown's West Coast Cook Book.* 1952. Rev. ed. New York: Alfred A. Knopf, 1991.

Brownlow, Kevin. *Hollywood: The Pioneers.* New York: Alfred A. Knopf, 1979.

Bullock, Paul, ed. *Watts, the Aftermath: An Inside View of the Ghetto by the People of Watts.* New York: Grove Press, 1972.

BIBLIOGRAPHY

Camarillo, Albert. *Chicanos in a Changing Society.* Cambridge: Harvard University Press, 1979.

Caughey, John, and LaRee Caughey. *Los Angeles: Biography of a City.* Berkeley: University of California Press, 1976.

Cho, Jenny. *Chinatown in Los Angeles.* Los Angeles: Arcadia Publishing, 2009.

Cleland, Robert Glass. *The Cattle on a Thousand Hills: Southern California, 1850–1880.* 1941. Reprint. San Marino: Huntington Library, 2005.

Cuero, Delfina. *The Autobiography of Delfina Cuero: A Diegueño Indian.* Los Angeles: Dawson's Book Shop, 1968.

Dana, Richard Henry. *Two Years Before the Mast.* 1840. Reprint. New York: Dodd, Mead & Co., 1946.

Daniels, Roger. *Prisoners Without Trial: Japanese Americans in World War II.* New York: Hill & Wang, 1993.

Didion, Joan. *Play It As It Lays.* New York: Farrar, Straus & Giroux, 1970.

Dinkelspiel, Frances. *Towers of Gold: How One Jewish Immigrant Named Isaac Hellman Created California.* St. Martin's Press, 2008.

Drain, Thomas A., and David Wakely. *A Sense of Mission: Historic Churches of the Southwest.* San Francisco: Chronicle Books, 1994.

du Petit-Thouars, Abel. *Voyage of the Venus: Sojourn in California.* Early California Travels Series, Vol. 35. Los Angeles: Glen Dawson, 1956.

Ellenbecker, John G. *The Jayhawkers of Death Valley.* 1938. Rev. ed. Marysville, Kans.: Privately printed, 1993.

Gioia, Ted. *West Coast Jazz: Modern Jazz in California, 1945-1960.* New York and Oxford: Oxford University Press, 1992.

Goldberg, George. *East Meets West: The Story of the Chinese and Japanese in California.* New York: Harcourt Brace Jovanovich, 1970.

BIBLIOGRAPHY

Griswold del Castillo, Richard. *La Familia: Chicano Families in the Urban Southwest, 1848 to the Present.* Notre Dame: University of Notre Dame, 1984.

Higa, Karin M. *The View from Within: Japanese American Art from the Internment Camps, 1942–1945.* Los Angeles: Japanese American National Museum, UCLA Wight Gallery, and UCLA Asian American Studies Center, 1992.

Hogeland, L. Frank, and Kim Hogeland. *First Families: Photographic History of California Indians.* Berkeley: Heyday Books, 2007.

Jaeger, Edmund C. *The California Deserts.* 4th ed. Stanford: Stanford University Press, 1965.

James, Harry C. *The Cahuilla Indians.* Los Angeles: Westernlore Press, 1960.

Jensen, Joan M., and Gloria Ricci Lothrop. *California Women: A History.* San Francisco: Boyd & Fraser, 1987.

Kitano, Harry H. *Japanese Americans: The Evolution of a Subculture.* 2nd ed. Englewood Cliffs, N.J.: Prentice-Hall, 1976.

Klein, Norman M. *The History of Forgetting: Los Angeles and the Erasure of Memory.* Updated ed. New York: Verso Books, 2008.

Krauss, Erich. *Wall of Flame: The Heroic Battle to Save Southern California.* New York: Wiley, 2006.

Lavender, David. *California: Land of New Beginnings.* New York: Harper & Row, 1972.

Malone, Michael P. and Richard W. Etulain. *The American West: A Twentieth-Century History.* Lincoln: University of Nebraska, 1989.

McWilliams, Carey. *Southern California Country: An Island on the Land.* New York: Duell, Sloan & Pearce, 1946.

Pearce, T. M. *Mary Hunter Austin.* United States Authors Series. New York: Twayne Publishers, 1965.

Picturing California: A Century of Photographic Genius. San Francisco: Chronicle Books/The Oakland Museum, 1989.

Pitt, Leonard. *Decline of the Californios: A Social History of the Spanish-Speaking Californians, 1846–1890.* Berkeley: University of California Press, 1999.

Pomeroy, Earl. *The Pacific Slope: A History of California, Oregon, Washington, Idaho, Utah, and Nevada.* New York: Alfred A. Knopf, 1965.

Rolle, Andrew F. *California: A History.* New York: Thomas Y. Cromwell, 1963.

Roske, Ralph J. *Everyman's Eden: A History of California.* New York: Macmillan, 1968.

Sackman, Douglas Cazaux. *Orange Empire: California and the Fruits of Eden.* Berkeley: University of California Press, 2007.

Sklar, Robert. *Movie-Made America: A Cultural History of American Movies.* New York: Random House, 1975.

Starr, Kevin. *Americans and the California Dream, 1850–1915.* New York: Oxford University Press, 1973.

_____. *Golden Dreams: California in an Age of Abundance.* New York: Oxford University Press, 2009.

_____. *Inventing the Dream: California through the Progressive Era.* New York: Oxford University Press, 1985.

_____. *Material Dreams: Southern California through the 1920s.* New York: Oxford University Press, 1990.

Storer, Tracy I., and Lloyd P. Tevis, Jr. *California Grizzly.* Berkeley: University of California Press, 1955.

Vorspan, Max and Lloyd P. Gartner. *History of the Jews of Los Angeles.* San Marino, Calif.: Huntington Library, 1970.

Wattawa, Gayle, ed. *Inlandia: A Literary Journey Through California's Inland Empire.* Berkeley: Heyday Books, 2006.

Weaver, John D. *El Pueblo Grande: A Non-Fiction Book about Los Angeles.* Los Angeles: The Ward Ritchie Press, 1973.

Worster, Donald. *Rivers of Empire: Water, Aridity, and the Growth of the American West.* New York: Pantheon Books, 1985.

INDEX

INDEX

INDEX

INDEX

ABOUT THE AUTHOR

Noelle Sullivan has written essays, poems, stories, and several small books of history. She holds a master's degree in the history of the American West from the University of New Mexico. Her work includes contributions to *The New Montana Story* and *M-e Ecci Aashi Awadi: The Knife River Indian Villages*. She lives in Montana with her husband and three daughters, and writes for the blog Montana Gael.